BARNEY KESSEL

A Step-by-Step Breakdown of His Guitar Styles and Techniques
by Wolf Marshall

PLAYBACK+
Speed • Pitch • Balance • Loop

To access audio visit:
www.halleonard.com/mylibrary

Enter Code
6925-1671-3326-3346

Cover photo by David Redfern/Redferns/Getty Images

ISBN: 978-1-4234-3047-6

HAL•LEONARD®

Visit Hal Leonard Online at
www.halleonard.com

Contact us:
Hal Leonard
7777 West Bluemound Road
Milwaukee, WI 53213
Email: info@halleonard.com

In Europe, contact:
Hal Leonard Europe Limited
42 Wigmore Street
Marylebone, London, W1U 2RN
Email: info@halleonardeurope.com

In Australia, contact:
Hal Leonard Australia Pty. Ltd.
4 Lentara Court
Cheltenham, Victoria, 3192 Australia
Email: info@halleonard.com.au

CONTENTS

FOREWORD

Barney Kessel holds special memories for me. Growing up in Los Angeles in the late sixties, I was aware of his legendary status when I first became interested in guitar. His name and reputation preceded him. Barney played on a ton of records across the musical spectrum, from T-Bone Walker and Charlie Parker to Julie London and Ricky Nelson. And he had a flashy red Gibson guitar named after him. That's potent stuff for any aspiring guitar kid.

If all that weren't enough, anyone who was anyone was hanging out at Barney Kessel's Music World on Yucca Street—just across the road from the famed Capitol Tower building in Hollywood, amidst all the old Hollywood landmarks and a stone's throw from the Musician's Union Local 47 on Vine Street. Unlike many of the stores in the area, Barney's shop was a haven for wayward players and welcomed seasoned pros, working musicians, super stars and starry-eyed students alike. John Lennon, George Harrison, and Eric Clapton are known to have shopped there, shoulder to shoulder with moms and dads buying junior their first guitar. In fact, no guitar player's walking tour of downtown Hollywood in the late sixties was complete without a visit to Barney Kessel's Music World.

A few years later, I began exploring music beyond my rock, pop, and blues roots and discovered Barney's playing on the *Poll Winners Three!* album. Upon first listen, I was captivated by his energetic improvisations, strong rhythmic drive, unflagging sense of swing, and sophisticated chord-melody approach. Barney's ability to squeeze that much music out of the guitar was remarkable, impressive, and appealing. Here was a picker who transformed six strings and twenty frets into a portable orchestra or big band. Accompanied only by bass and drums, Barney filled the musical space as no one I had heard to this point. Moreover, he was musically adventurous and freely exploited a wide variety of textures and unusual sound effects in addition to the requisite traditional single-note jazz and blues licks and chord-melody passages. I believe Barney was the first guitarist I heard to use bi-dextral effects, slapped harmonics, extensive sweep picking, percussive noises, and tap-on bass lines. The aforementioned qualities and his strong individuality continue to resound in Barney's music for the ages, inspiring future generations of listeners and players. We salute you, Maestro Kessel!

—Wolf Marshall

Post script: Your humble author had the privilege and pleasure to spend quality time with the master in the years before his death. Barney's ability to speak and articulate may have been diminished somewhat, but his desire to communicate and to share the intricacies of music certainly was not. A devoted music lover to the end, Barney filled his final months listening to the sounds he embraced throughout his life and cataloging earlier live recordings for posterity. Though impaired physically, Barney exuded an enthusiasm, joy of discovery, and love of the art form, perhaps rivaled only by the starry-eyed students who once gathered at Barney Kessel's Music World.

INTRODUCTION

This entry in the Guitar Signature Licks series is dedicated to the sounds and techniques of Barney Kessel. Barney is a guitarist who is acclaimed as an important transitional figure, one who was pivotal—essential—in the jazz genre as the music evolved past its swing roots into bebop, hard bop, and modern jazz.

The selections in this volume are gathered from, arguably, his most significant and influential period: the 1950s, when jazz guitar was still in its infancy. Several pieces are presented in their entirety: "Tenderly," "Salute to Charlie Christian," "Speak Low," and three *Poll Winners* trio tunes, "Minor Mood," "Foreign Intrigue," and "I'm Afraid the Masquerade Is Over." These are guitar intensive arrangements that showcase Barney's guitar role prominently and must be studied as complete works. Listen to the whole track and follow along with the detailed analysis of the distinct sections. Others, like "Barney's Blues," "Indiana," and "64 Bars on Wilshire," are offered in specific sections, where the guitar is stating the theme, interacting with the ensemble, or featured as the solo instrument.

The time codes displayed in the selections refer to the original recordings.

BIOGRAPHY

Barney Kessel is one of the most famed and beloved jazz guitarists in music history. To many aficionados, his name is synonymous with jazz guitar. Bred on swing music of the 1940s, Kessel was one of the earliest players to absorb the language of modern jazz and bebop, mixing the new and old sounds with a swinging delivery, rhythmic vitality, and musical imagination all his own. His work remains towering and influential to the present, and he is widely acknowledged as one the leading voices of jazz guitar.

Born in Muskogee, Oklahoma, on October 17, 1923, Barney Kessel decided on a career in music at an early age. He bought his first guitar at age twelve with money saved from selling newspapers. Essentially self-taught, Kessel received a few rudimentary lessons in a Federal Music Program of the WPA in the summer of 1935. His earliest influences included swing musicians Charlie Christian (guitar) and Lester Young (tenor sax). Over the next four years, Kessel progressed quickly and established a strong regional following, enhanced by performances with the Varsitonians, a twelve-piece college band, while still a young teenager.

By 1939, Kessel's reputation had grown to the point that his mentor Charlie Christian sought him out during a visit back home (Oklahoma was also Christian's home state). At age sixteen, Kessel met, hung out, and jammed with his idol, a duly impressed Christian, in early October of 1940. This experience inspired him to pursue a full-time professional career in music.

In 1942, Kessel moved to Los Angeles and worked as a dishwasher while he made the musical rounds, sought auditions, and developed contacts. He was soon hired to play in comedian Chico Marx's band, led by drummer Ben Pollock. Kessel rapidly became a major player in the burgeoning West Coast jazz scene, performing and recording with Charlie Parker, Howard McGhee, Wardell Gray, Sonny Criss, and many others. Like many jazz musicians of the era, he also began accepting studio work on radio networks and Hollywood film scores and joined Frank De Vol's commercial orchestra.

In 1944, Kessel appeared in Norman Granz's award-winning jazz documentary *Jammin' the Blues*. He was the only white musician in the film. Kessel also played in numerous big bands between 1945 and 1947, including the ensembles of Charlie Barnet and Artie Shaw. Kessel performed on record dates with Shorty Rogers and Benny Goodman, toured with the Oscar Peterson Trio in 1951–1952, and participated in Norman Granz's prestigious *Jazz at the Philharmonic* concert series. His contributions to Charlie Parker's legacy, contained in important tracks from 1947 like "Carvin' the Bird" and "Relaxin at Camarillo," brought further acclaim and broadened his jazz credentials. These and other high profile concerts and recordings led to Kessel's greater exposure and recognition in America and Europe.

Kessel began recording as a leader in 1953 on the LA-based Contemporary label. His earliest releases remain eternal jazz guitar classics and have influenced countless players to follow. These albums capture Kessel at the height of his powers, accompanied by sterling musicians like Hampton Hawes, Red Mitchell, Harry "Sweets" Edison, Andre Previn, Bud Shank, Buddy Collette, Victor Feldman, Ben Webster, Art Pepper, Leroy Vinegar, Monty Budwig, and Jack Marshall. Kessel's Contemporary sessions boasted his attractive blues-based jazz guitar style and showcased his original compositions and arrangements.

Kessel topped all the major polls in the late fifties, including the Downbeat Readers Poll (1956–1959), the *Playboy* Readers Poll (1957–1960), and the *Metronome* Readers Poll (1958–1960) as well as those in *Esquire* and *Melody Maker*. His popular success and credentials led directly to a fortuitous partnership with bassist Ray Brown and drummer Shelley Manne, chronicled on the renowned *Poll Winners* albums. Their efforts, begun in 1957, are the earliest studio recordings of note to exploit the now-standard guitar/bass/drums trio combination and are enduring classics of jazz.

Kessel's list of recording credits is immense and diverse. A partial tally includes illustrious names like Billie Holiday, Charlie Parker, Ella Fitzgerald, Frank Sinatra, Sarah Vaughan, Bing Crosby, Art Tatum, T-Bone Walker, Duane Eddy, Liberace, Kid Ory, Bobby Hutcherson, Lester Young, Judy Garland, Lionel Hampton, Sonny Rollins, Oscar Peterson, Julie London, Elvis Presley, Mel Torme, Sam Cooke, Hampton Hawes, Stephane Grappelli, Roy Eldridge, Ben Webster, Woody Herman, Red Norvo, Stuff Smith, George Wein's Newport All Stars, Andre Previn, the Coasters, the Beach Boys, Cher, the Righteous Brothers, and many others. Kessel's studio credentials also include prominent TV scores like *Perry Mason* and *I Spy,* production work for rock 'n' roll singer Ricky Nelson, and a stint as A&R man for Verve Records.

In the late sixties, Kessel developed a notable presence as an educator. He was one of the first jazz guitarists to focus on music education, conducting worldwide seminars (*The Effective Guitarist*), publishing the Barney Kessel Personal Manuscript series, and penning the substantial reference tome *The Guitar* (1967). In the ensuing years, Kessel wrote a tutorial method for guitar, contributed a regular column for *Guitar Player* magazine, and produced four instructional videos.

In 1969, Kessel left the commercial studio scene permanently to concentrate solely on his jazz career. He subsequently toured the globe, playing numerous festivals and club gigs, relocated briefly to London, and performed regularly as leader and accompanist. At this time, Kessel was appointed Ambassador of Jazz and served in this capacity for the US State Department.

In 1973, Kessel teamed up with fretboard cohorts Charlie Byrd and Herb Ellis to form The Great Guitars group, the first working ensemble fronted by three influential jazz guitarists. The trio performed regularly until 1992, when Kessel suffered a debilitating stroke and partial paralysis that forced him to retire from public performance. He settled in the San Diego area with his lovely and elegant wife Phyllis Van Doren and worked with selected students for the rest of his life.

Kessel was diagnosed with inoperable cancer in 2001 and left us in May of 2004. He was eighty years old. A testament to his love and commitment, Kessel remained connected and fully engaged with music until the very end, despite his infirmity. His final years found him involved with cataloging his music—especially his unreleased live recordings. Ever gracious and aware of his legacy, Kessel also granted interviews on a limited basis at this time. One of these appeared in part in my *Best of Charlie Christian* Guitar Signature Licks book, wherein he described important details about Christian's style and technique and his time spent with the first electric jazz guitarist.

One of the all-time greats of modern music, Barney Kessel will long be remembered for his inimitable sense of swing and rhythmic drive, his fiery improvisations, colorful chord-melody style, and his many lasting contributions to the jazz art form. These contributions transcended the jazz genre and affected players in rock, R&B, country, blues, fusion, and popular music, and are forever embedded in the landscape of Americana.

THE BARNEY KESSEL SOUND

The Barney Kessel sound is immediately recognizable. And while his style and vision continued to evolve throughout his lifetime, his stringy tone, well-accented bebop lines, and soulful blues bite have been delivered by a familiar and reliable iconic instrument: the guitar that has been his constant companion since his earliest professional years.

In an illuminating videotaped interview, currently included on the Vestapol DVD *Rare Performances*, Kessel expounded on his personal instrument and its unique attributes. He stated that he had been playing the same guitar, a Gibson ES-350P, since 1947. The ES-350P (Premier) was the company's first arch-top electric with a cutaway. Kessel's has a deep (3 3/8-inch) hollow body and a sunburst finish and was equipped with a single pickup in the neck position.

Over the years, Kessel made several purposeful modifications to his ES-350. At the outset, he opted for a "Charlie Christian" bar pickup instead of the stock P-90 single-coil pickup. He removed the tortoise shell pickguard early on. By the mid-fifties, Kessel had changed the original rosewood fingerboard with double-parallelogram inlays to an ebony board with dot inlays. This was seen on the cover of his first album *Easy Like* (1953). He also fitted his 350 with a high-quality ebony bridge built along violin standards.

Kessel later upgraded the stock open-back tuning keys with Keystone plastic buttons: first to Grover Imperials and then to gold-plated Schaller type. He replaced the original Gibson speed knobs with black chicken-head control knobs with pointers, allegedly scrounged from an old radio. He specified that these knobs allowed him to preset volume and tone easily by feel, even in the dark or under the brightest stage lights. Moreover, Kessel repainted the headstock, obscuring the original manufacturer name.

To emphasize the treble strings, Kessel adjusted his bar pickup at an angle. He used a heavy pick and preferred Darco medium-heavy-gauge round-wound strings. Kessel favored no specific amplifier and used various Gibson, Fender, and Univox models throughout his career.

DISCOGRAPHY

The titles in this volume are found on the following recordings.

EASY LIKE: BARNEY KESSEL, VOLUME 1—Contemporary C-3511 (OJCD-153-2): "Easy Like," "Tenderly," "Vicky's Dream," "Salute to Charlie Christian."

KESSEL PLAYS STANDARDS: BARNEY KESSEL, VOLUME 2—Contemporary C-3512 (OJCD-238-2): "Speak Low," "On a Slow Boat to China," " Barney's Blues," "64 Bars on Wilshire."

TO SWING OR NOT TO SWING: BARNEY KESSEL, VOLUME 3—Contemporary C-3513 8276 (OJCD -317-2): "Begin the Blues," "Indiana," "Contemporary Blues."

THE POLL WINNERS—Contemporary S-7535 (OJCD-156-2): "Minor Mood."

THE POLL WINNERS RIDE AGAIN!—Contemporary S-7556 (OJCD-607-2): "Foreign Intrigue."

POLL WINNERS THREE!—Contemporary S-7576 (OJCD-692-2): "I'm Afraid the Masquerade Is Over."

THE RECORDING

Wolf Marshall: guitar
Robert Parker: piano
Bob Magnusson: bass
Mike Sandberg: drums, percussion
John Rekevics: tenor saxophone on "Vicky's Dream" and "64 Bars on Wilshire"
Roland Coltrane Orchestra: additional sax, trumpet, and oboe

Special thanks to Gary Rico

Music transcriptions by Wolf Marshall

EASY LIKE

(Easy Like: Barney Kessel, Volume 1)
By Barney Kessel

Figure 1—Head

Barney Kessel dominated the jazz guitar world of the fifties. His apprenticeship in swing bands of the forties and involvement with jazz giants like Charlie Parker, Wardell Gray, and Oscar Peterson paved the way for his formal emergence as a leader in 1953. By the mid-fifties, Kessel had grown into a respected and recognized solo artist.

Based in Los Angeles, Kessel was the leading guitarist of the West Coast jazz scene. As his reputation grew, Kessel scored an exclusive record contract with Contemporary Records. His fifties output, arguably his most influential work, captured on a series of superb Contemporary albums, is widely acknowledged as a turning point in modern jazz guitar.

One of the most identifiable soloists of the still-new electric guitar, Kessel crafted a distinctive sound from blues, bebop, and swing elements. That's what listeners were treated to with his first Contemporary releases. The debut album, *Easy Like: Barney Kessel, Volume 1*, featured tracks from 1953–1956. It combined material from three recording sessions originally issued as EPs (Extended Play), 10-inch records, on Onyx and Verve. The title track, Barney Kessel's original composition "Easy Like," was recorded in Los Angeles on February 23, 1956, during the last of the three studio dates. Participating in the session were Red Mitchell (bass), Buddy Collette (flute), Claude Williamson (piano), and Shelly Manne (drums), all fixtures of the West Coast jazz scene.

"Easy Like" begins with Kessel's attractive down-home theme. The catchy guitar line in the [A] section of the head reflects his personal mix of Oklahoma-bred country-tinged blues and uptown jazz harmony, striking a balance of the soulful and cerebral. Here, Kessel adopts a fingerstyle approach to the polyphonic theme phrases, interpolating a simple walking bass line below the sparse blues melody.

Kessel's theme is made of three iterations of the blues-based F–F#°–C/G progression followed by contrasting phrases of greater harmonic and contrapuntal content: A7#5♭9–Am11–D13–G13, enlivened with contrary and parallel motion. During the second half, the Dm7–G7#5–C cadence progression in measures 9–10 receives a subtle contrapuntal treatment with country-blues implications and contrary and parallel motion.

In the [B] section (measures 12–26), Kessel plays a more homophonic variation of the theme, a pianistic chordal figure rendered with claw-style articulation. He plucks the upper-partial tritone dyad (A and E♭) while posing a low-register melody underneath. Kessel retains the harmony from the main theme while unfolding a new melody, as in the standard blues form, and repeats chord progressions and polyphonic figures heard from the first [A] section in measures 17–19 and 25–26.

Fig. 1   **3**   Full Band

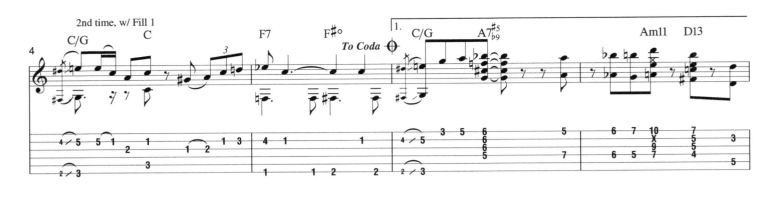

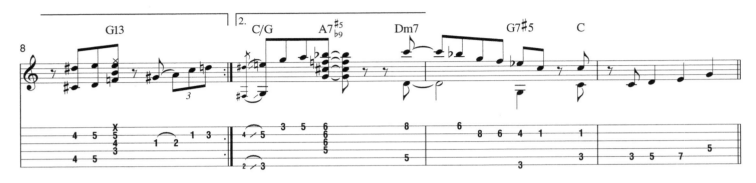

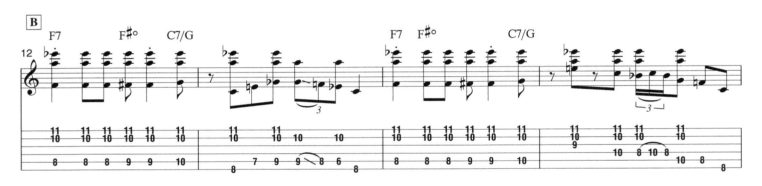

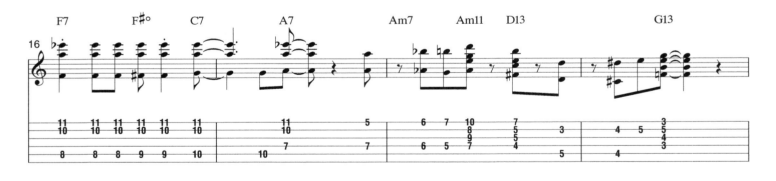

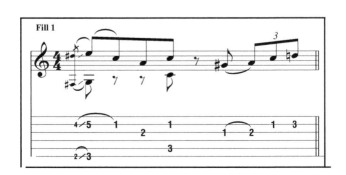

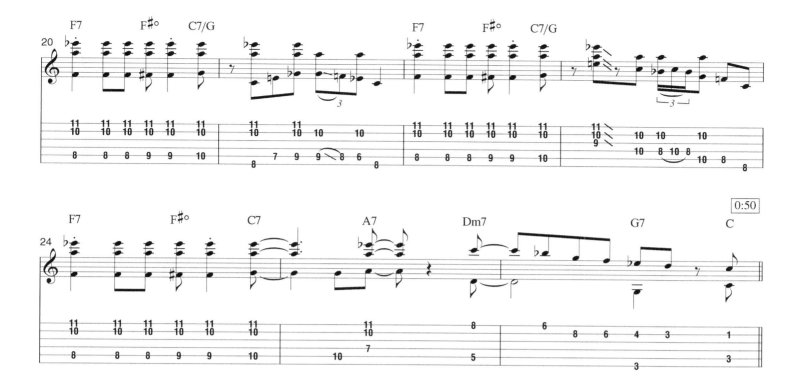

Figure 2—Guitar Solo, Recap and Coda

Kessel's guitar solo C in "Easy Like" exemplifies his early bebop style. Played over the tune's cycling chord progression, it conveys his marriage of blues, bop, and swing idioms. Alongside many references to his role models, guitarist Charlie Christian and tenor saxophonist Lester Young, are heady lines gleaned from Charlie "Bird" Parker and Dizzy Gillespie, as well as funky blues licks of rural origin.

Kessel begins his solo with a blues-based pickup break. He plays both articulated and held bends in measures 1–4 and places these in context within the C blues scale. By contrast, his lines in measures 6–8 are chord-related and laced with bop chromaticism. Note the imitative melodies over D7 and G7. Kessel adopts a riff-oriented approach over F7–F#°–C/G in measures 9–13, milking three simple C minor figures, distinguished by use of the 9th (D) and 6th (A) tones and blues ornaments. He closes the first half with a C minor pentatonic line over the Dm7–G7–C cadence.

Kessel pursues blues sounds and string bends in measures 16–20. Note the use of half-step string bends starting on D and A, the 9th and 6th degrees—operative tones of the swing genre. This procedure, in effect, adds those tones to Kessel's pentatonic framework. In measure 22, Kessel reprises a snippet of the lick heard earlier in measure 6 before launching into a complex double-timed line in measures 23–24. This longer intricate passage in consistent sixteenth notes is typical of Kessel's bebop side. It is informed by Bird and distinguished by idiomatic chromaticism, chord-related interval leaps, encircling figures, and slurred phrasing. The melody played on beats 3 and 4 of measure 23 is a favorite Kessel motive used often in similar bop lines. The complex bebop passage leads seamlessly to simpler blues and groove riffs in measures 25–27.

Kessel's final thoughts include rhythmically animated lines. Note his major-blues phrase in measure 28, a sequence of F major and F# diminished arpeggios in sixteenth notes in measure 29, and a bebop-inflected line fragmented by rests over C–A7–Dm7–G7 changes in measures 30–31.

The recap is a truncated version of the head. Kessel and company play the first sixteen measures of A verbatim before proceeding to a brief coda. This final section finds him repeating the theme's contrapuntal Dm7–G7–C phrase as a tag E. The spaces between his guitar phrases in measures 35–37 are filled with improvised upright bass licks. The final chord is a favorite Kessel voicing: a five-note Cmaj9/G, facilitated by *thumb fretting* across the sixth *and* fifth strings.

Fig. 2

C Guitar Solo 2:32

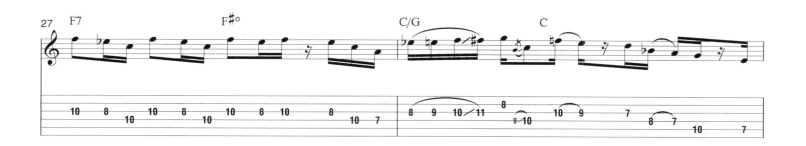

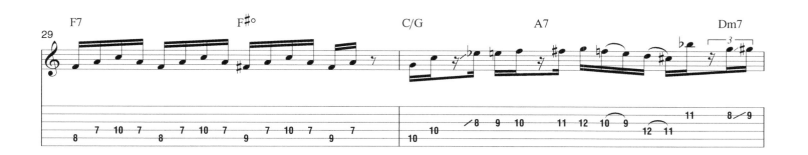

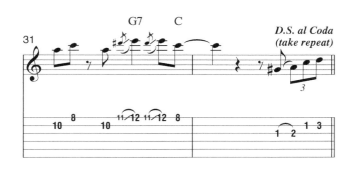

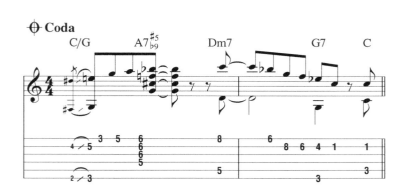

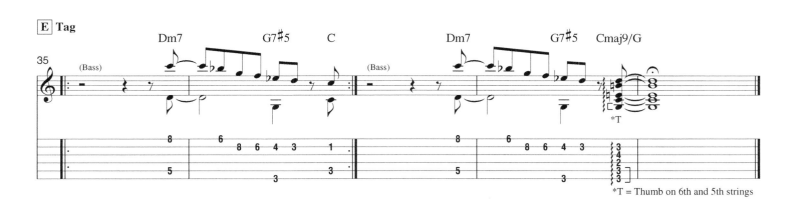

*T = Thumb on 6th and 5th strings

TENDERLY
from TORCH SONG
(*Easy Like: Barney Kessel, Volume 1*)
Lyric by Jack Lawrence
Music by Walter Gross

Figure 3—Head

"Tenderly," the beautiful evergreen standard, provided an ideal venue for Kessel's multifarious guitar approach. The guitar-dominated arrangement was recorded on November 14, 1953, and featured supportive accompaniment from Arnold Ross (piano), Harry Babasin (bass), and Shelly Manne (drums). Kessel played the tune in the original key of E♭ and crafted an effective arrangement to showcase his chord-melody conception, in unaccompanied and ensemble contexts, as well as his interpretation of the melody and prowess in single-note jazz improvisation.

The head A is a colorful and sophisticated chordal statement of the song's theme. Kessel plays the entire thirty-two-measure ABAC form as a plectrum-style chord solo in free time. This section functions as a prelude in the arrangement and highlights his keen sense of modern harmony and command of guitar techniques. Note the first sonority of the song in measure 1, a D/E♭ *bi-tonal* chord rendered with his ubiquitous *thumb fretting.* Kessel employs similar thumb fretting on various enriched and altered chords like A♭9♯11/E♭, A♭13♭9, G7♯5, F13♭9/C, C7♭5♭9, and B♭7♭5♭9 in the head, and C13♭9, B♭13♭9, and E♭maj9/B♭ in the coda D. Moreover, he uses thumb fretting for the pedal point figures in measures 22–23 and elsewhere in the solo.

In addition to colorful enriched and altered chord sounds, Kessel employs unusual and prescient guitar techniques in "Tenderly." He decorates the A♭13♭9 in measure 3 with *artificial harmonics.* These are swept with a rapid arpeggiation of the right hand, accomplished by tracing the shape of the fingered chord and lightly touching the strings with the fingertip (or palm edge) and plectrum. Also notable is the *tap-on* passage in measure 14, in which Kessel sustains an F13♭9♭5 at the tenth position while tapping a chromatically-descending independent bass line on the sixth string. To put things in historical perspective, bear in mind this was played four years before Eddie Van Halen was born.

Other points of interest in the head include Kessel's unique cadential pattern in measure 7, which serves to delay the resolution to E♭ with an alternate Gm7–G♭maj7–C♭maj7/G♭–E5♯11 progression, the stylistic *cluster voicings* and polyphony of A♭m9 in measures 9 and 11 and B♭m9 in measure 20, and the flat-five substitute of E11 (Bm7/E), and an extended parallel 3rds passage for B♭7 in measures 15–16. The latter is a fixture of Kessel's style and appears often in both substitute and conventional forms in his repertory.

Fig. 3

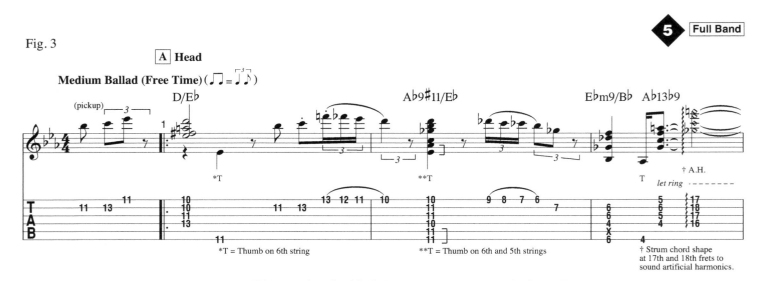

Figure 4—Guitar Solo and Outro

The first chorus of Kessel's guitar solo [B] strikes a balance between thematic development of the song's melody and unfettered jazz improvisation. It is played in a moderately slow swing groove that grows organically from the cadential figure in the second ending of the head, where the band enters and fixed time is established. Kessel alludes to the theme throughout measures 24–32, embellishing the original melody with repeated notes, slurs, rhythmic variations, ornamental figures, and harmonic extensions. Note the sequential passage in measures 28–30. This three-phrase line is based on the embellished melody fragment over Fm9 in measures 27–28 and is imitated on different scale degrees with harmonic adjustments for D♭9 and E♭maj7.

Kessel interpolates crammed double-timed bebop lines between his slower melody embellishments in measures 33–39. Note the Bird-inspired chromaticism, wide chord-tone leaps, and target/enclosure figures in his bop playing. The ii–V line in measures 38–39 (Fm7–B♭7) is particularly evocative. There, Kessel paraphrases one of Bird's favorite motives with similar sixteenth-note rhythm and chromatic patterns.

In the second half, Kessel creates a sequential phrase with imitative extended arpeggios for E♭maj7 and E♭m9 in measures 40–42. Note similar melodic contours and rhythm and the phrase's question-and-answer feeling. In this passage, Kessel follows the same strategy Bird used in the opening line of his "Just Friends" solo; check out *Charlie Parker with Strings*. Kessel switches to funky E♭ blues sounds and string bending over the changes in measures 44–47. He returns to his earlier strategy with thematic development of the song melody in measures 48 (A♭m9) and 50 (Cm7) separated by a double-timed bebop flurry over G7 in measure 49. Kessel closes the first chorus with a sequential turn-around pattern in measures 51–53 and a pedal point figure in measure 54, which alludes to the progression of descending diminished chords in the second ending of the head and signals a change in texture.

The second chorus [C] finds Kessel progressing to chord-melody playing in contrast to the single-note improvisations of the previous section. He plays the chords plectrum style and phrases many of the figures in the rhythmically charged manner of big band shout choruses. Note the use of thumb fretting throughout, quartal chords to harmonize a blues melody in measures 62–63, raked strums answered by octave figures in measures 64–67, and the alternation of triadic forms with larger sonorities in measures 68–71 and elsewhere. Kessel exploits *quartal chords* to connote E♭ and A♭7 in the triplet figures of measures 72–73. In measures 78–79, he superimposes a harmonically active and elusive substitute phrase of B♭m–C♭6/9–A♭–A7–A7♭5/B♭ over the normally expected static E♭ major chord.

Kessel returns to a single-note texture with an embellishment of the melody in measure 80 and a florid ascending line played with legato phrasing in measure 81. The final decorated song melody in measures 82–83 gives way to a brief coda, a four-measure outro again exploiting Kessel's unaccompanied chord-melody solo style.

The coda [D] consists of a iii–VI–ii–V progression distinguished by extended and altered chords and a final deceptive cadence. Kessel plays the latter in place of the expected E♭ tonic chord and utilizes the E♭ melody note as a pedal tone. Note the clever descending pattern and changing colors of the chords in the progression: G♭6–F7–Emaj7–A5♯11. The final sonority, an E♭maj9/B♭, is a favorite voicing and is facilitated by Kessel's expanded thumb fretting across the bass strings.

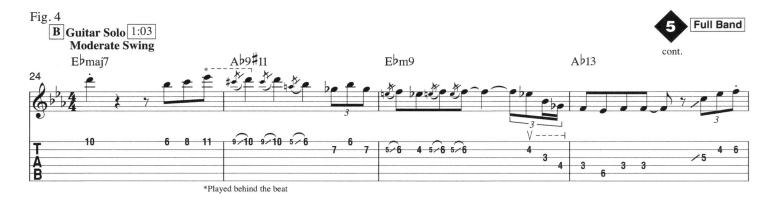

Fig. 4

[B] Guitar Solo 1:03
Moderate Swing

5 Full Band

cont.

*Played behind the beat

*Played behind the beat

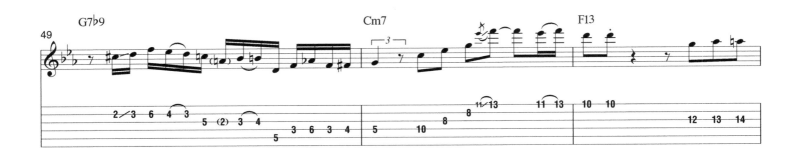

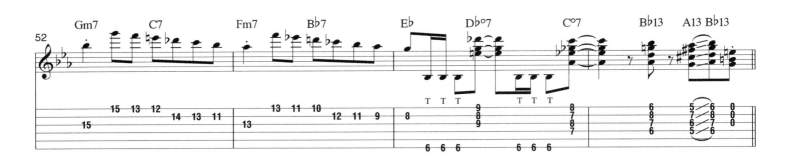

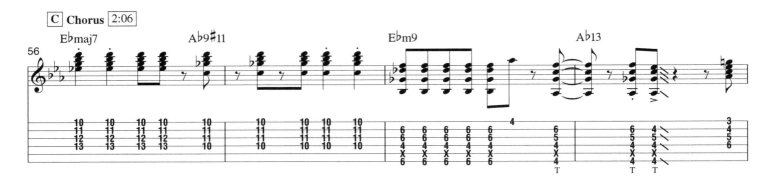

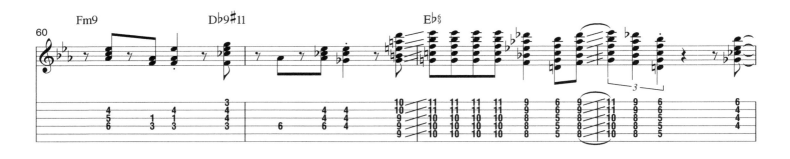

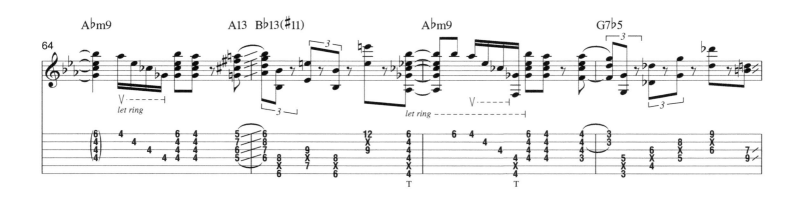

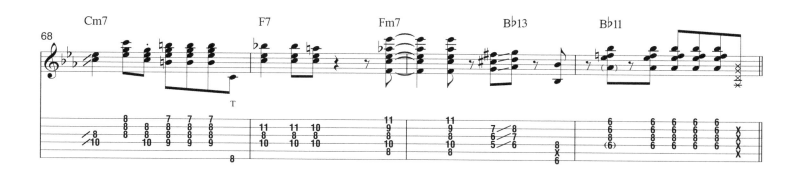

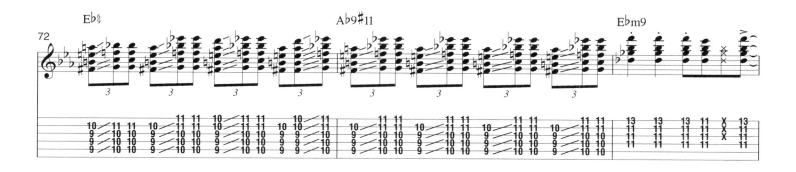

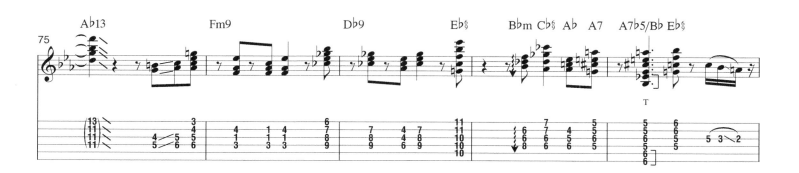

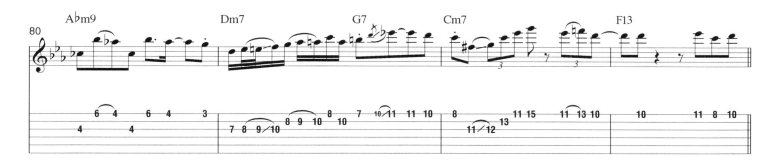

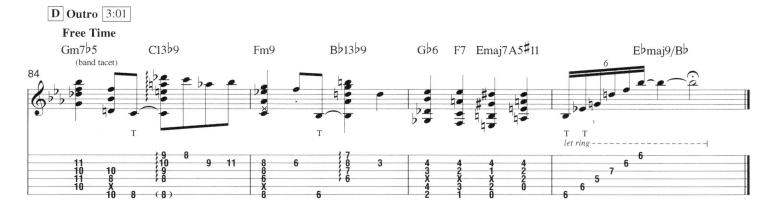

VICKY'S DREAM
(*Easy Like: Barney Kessel, Volume 1*)
By Barney Kessel

Figure 5—Intro and Head

"Vicky's Dream" was Barney Kessel's gift to the bebop world and a highlight of his debut album. This up-tempo original was recorded on November 14, 1953, in the same session and with the same personnel that produced "Tenderly." West Coast jazz stalwart Bud Shank augmented the lineup and contributed saxophone parts.

"Vicky's Dream" shares many characteristics common to the repertories of the great bebop masters, attesting to Kessel's fluency with the genre. It is a contrafact based on the chord changes of "All the Things You Are," a Jerome Kern standard well known and often played by jazz players in the milieu. Charlie Parker's "Bird of Paradise" was based on the same changes, as was Mal Waldron's "Anatomy," made famous by John Coltrane. Like the source version, "Vicky's Dream" is in the original key of A♭, utilizes the same larger thirty six-measure form, and exploits the same modulatory chord changes. Like Parker and Gillespie's take on the standard, Kessel adds a new independent intro section A to the form. Here, it is expressed as two hustling ii–V–I figures in A♭ major and F major, respectively.

Kessel's recomposed melody enters in measure 9, at the start of the head B. From the outset ,we hear the same melodic and rhythmic complexity and bebop phraseology that distinguished such contrafacts as "Donna Lee" and "Dexterity." We also find substantive harmonic digressions, like the superimposed Em7–A7 substitution (for E♭7) in measure 11 and the fluid minor chord motion in the bridge in measures 25–31. In the latter, Kessel develops a thematic scalar theme through the tonally unrelated changes of Am7–B♭m7– Bm7–F♯m7–Gm7–G♯m7.

Kessel plays a quirky whole-tone scale melody in parallel 3rds with the sax over the C7♯5 chord for a turnaround in measure 32. He further personalizes the tune with a chromatic progression of parallel minor-seventh chords in measures 39–41. Instead of the original A♭–A♭°–B♭m7 sheet-music pattern or the "Real Book changes" (Cm7–B°–B♭m7), Kessel's arrangement follows a Cm7–Bm7–B♭m7 progression. At the end of the head in measures 43–44, Kessel begins his solo with a two-measure pickup break implying A♭–C7.

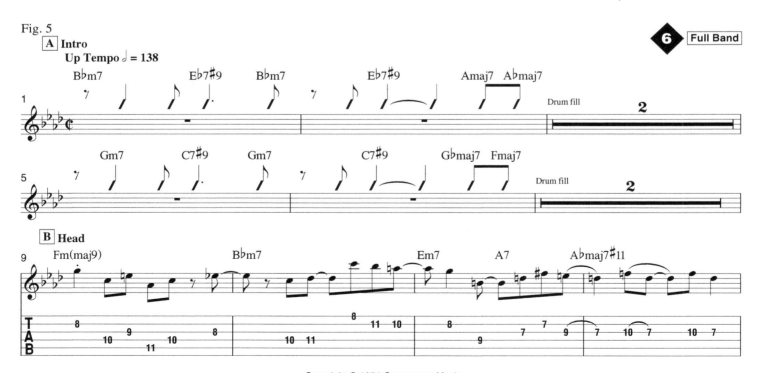

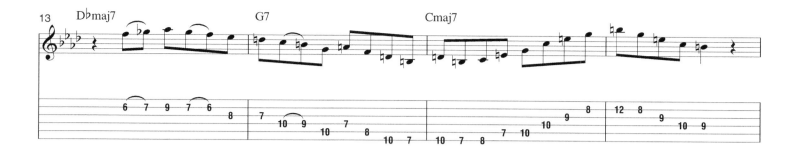
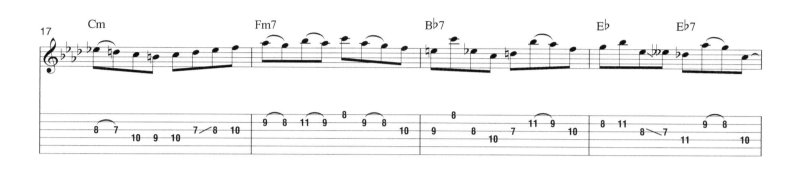
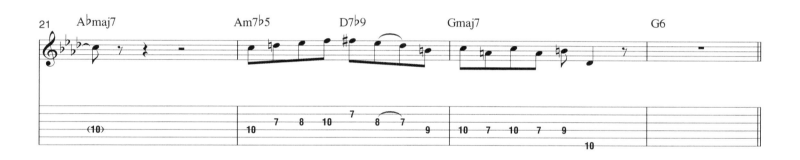

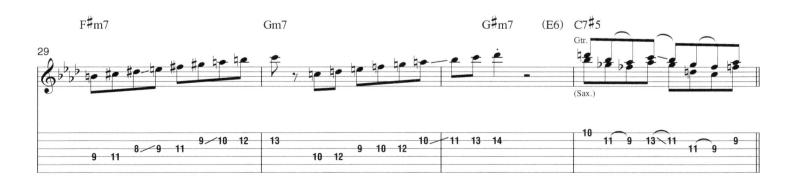

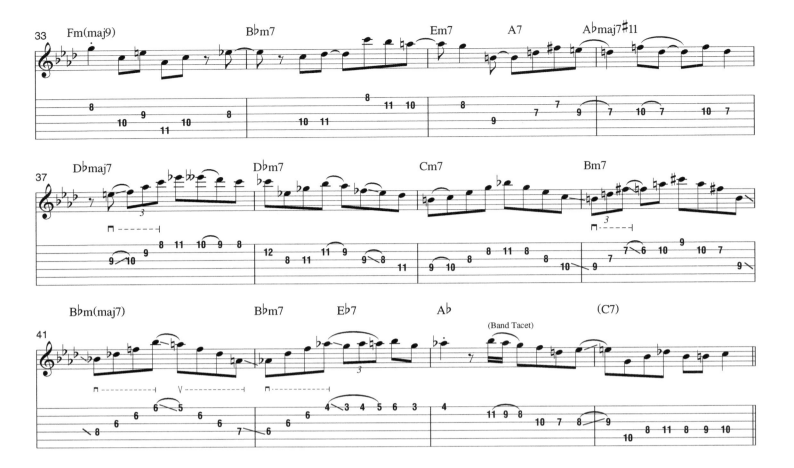

Figure 6—Guitar Solo

Kessel follows a thematic approach in his two-chorus solo. He opens his first chorus C with melodious sequential lines defining the *cycle-of-fourths* progression of measures 1–6. Note the observance of chord tones, similar melodic contours, the question-and-answer phraseology, and his adherence to the standard changes for blowing. Kessel develops arpeggio sounds in measures 8–12. Here, he outlines Cm7 and Fm7 with similar motives and varies the figure to connote B♭7♯5 in measure 11. In measures 13–15, Kessel mixes arpeggios with chromatic tones. Note similar triad shapes used for A♭6 and Gmaj7.

Kessel works another motive of 7th interval leaps and quick descending arpeggios for the Am7–D7–Gmaj7 changes in measures 16–19. Note his use of a Cm9 sound as a substitute for the altered D7 in measure 18. Kessel echoes this phrase with slight melodic alterations in E for the F♯m7–B7–Emaj7 changes in measures 20–24.

Kessel finishes the chorus with rhythmic ideas and ostinatos. He repeats an insistent A♭ tone in a steady quarter-note pulse in measures 25–28 and then uses the tone to build a series of riff-oriented figures over the changes in measures 28–32. Note the simple descending half-step motion to accommodate the riffs over the chromatic progression of D♭–D♭m7–Cm7–Bm7. Kessel closes with a bebop line over the final ii–V–I (B♭m7–E♭7–A♭maj7) in measures 33–35. Check out the chromatic passing tones, arpeggio outlines, altered-chord melody, and repeated figures in this phrase.

In the second chorus D, Kessel adopts a more impassioned approach to the first half. Many of his most identifiable traits are found in this section. Note the raked figures in measures 38 and 41, which are embellished with slurred articulation and legato phrasing. Kessel plays bebop melodies in measures 38–41 and a long, largely eighth-note based line in measures 46–51. Note the characteristic bop approach tones, target notes, interval leaps, and altered-chord melody. Moreover, the phrase ending in measures 43–44 is an absolute staple of the bebop language. Here, Kessel implies an *altered chord* sound (G7♭9) over Cmaj7 and colors the descending line with major 7th and 6th tones in a specific melodic configuration.

Kessel returns to a thematic approach in the bridge for measures 53–60. As he did earlier, he establishes a four-bar phrase in G in measures 53–56 and presents a variant in E in measures 57–59. Kessel combines and expounds on sounds introduced earlier in his final thoughts. Note the bebop elements in the long line of measures 61–64 and the riff-based treatment of *extended arpeggio* melodies in measures 65–69. The latter passage conforms to the chromatic descending progression of minor chords, as before. Kessel wraps up his solo in the bop vein with an energetic line laced with functional chromaticism, characteristic chord-related figures, and horn-like phrasing. Case in point is the final lick in measures 72–73. This is straight out of the Charlie Parker playbook, with its implicit altered scale sound (C7#5♭9), defining interval jump (E–G), and diminished arpeggio (G–B♭–D♭).

Fig. 6

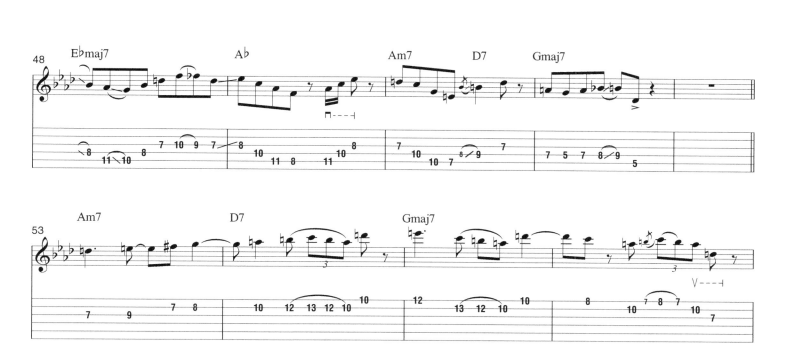

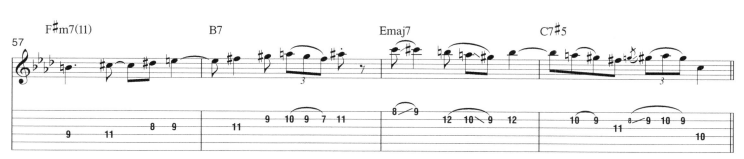

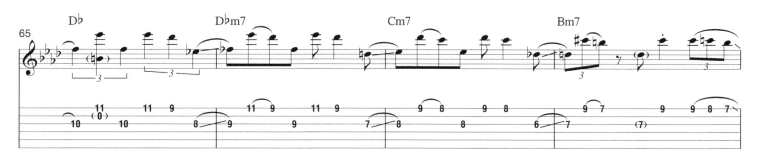

SALUTE TO CHARLIE CHRISTIAN

(*Easy Like: Barney Kessel, Volume 1*)
By Barney Kessel

Figure 7—Intro and Head

Barney Kessel is widely heralded as the most visible and influential player in the first wave of the post-Charlie Christian jazz guitarists. Of the players surfacing in the late forties and early fifties, like Tal Farlow, Jimmy Raney, Herb Ellis, Kenny Burrell, Howard Roberts, and Jim Hall, Kessel came closest to capturing the musical ethos of Christian, down to his soulful blues mannerisms, swinging eighth-note lines, deliberate rhythmic punctuations, and command of essential swing-era clichés. And it's no wonder; they both shared the same folksy Oklahoma roots, strived for a horn-like approach to single-note improvisation, honored rhythm as a priority, and came of age as jazz became America's popular music. It is only fitting that his first album featured an ode to his idol and musical role model.

"Salute to Charlie Christian" is just that: an acknowledgement in musical terms of the lessons learned listening to the archetype electric jazz guitarist. Kessel repaid debts owed in full with this outstanding tribute, an original composition recorded on December 19, 1953. The blues-based minor-mode piece embodies the excitement and drama of Christian's style without undue imitation and repurposes the jazz language of the swing era without artifice. As such, it is replete with Charlie Christian signature sounds that found new expression in Kessel's early bebop palette.

"Salute to Charlie Christian" is a musical mosaic that reconciles minor blues, AABA standards, and "Rhythm changes." The arrangement begins with an eight-measure rhythm section intro with four measures of swinging drum groove at the top. Piano and bass enter in the second half. The intro establishes the main harmonic theme with its vamped minor-mode progression of B♭m–B♭m/A♭–G♭6 (or B♭m/G♭)–F7, similar to now familiar pieces like Ray Charles' "Hit the Road, Jack" and Brian Setzer's "Stray Cat Strut."

The song features a thirty-two-measure AABA form in B♭ minor with a set melody, akin to a truncated minor blues, in the A sections and an open eight-measure bridge, somewhat like "Rhythm changes." The latter section follows a B♭7–E♭7–A♭7–D♭6–Cm7♭5–F7 progression, combining the cycle-of-fourths in dominant-seventh chords of "I Got Rhythm" with a ♭III–ii–V cadence in B♭ minor. To this structure, Kessel applies a central blues-based melody of call-and-response phrases over the vamped changes in the A sections. During the first sixteen measures of the head [A], the theme melody is stated twice in B♭ minor (first [A], eight measures) and then once in E♭ minor and B♭ minor (second [A]), like the i and iv chords of a minor blues. Kessel plays chord-related improvisatory lines in [B] sections. The final A section recaps the first eight measures of the theme.

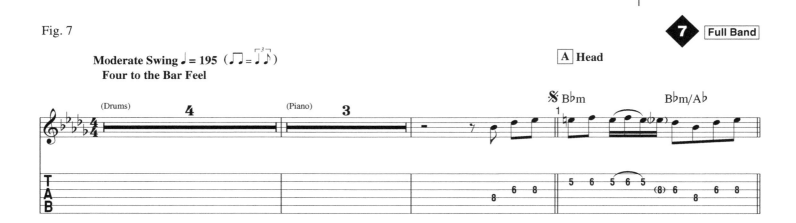

Fig. 7

Moderate Swing ♩ = 195 (♫ = ♩♪)
Four to the Bar Feel

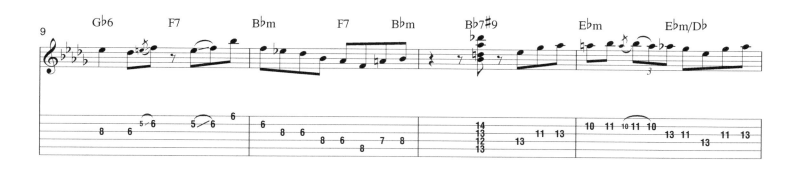

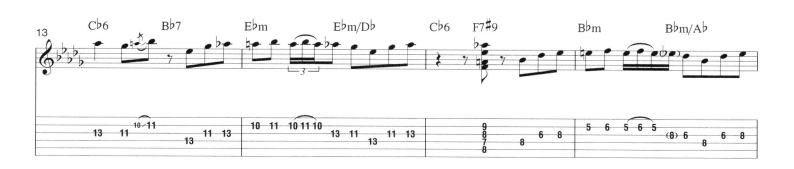

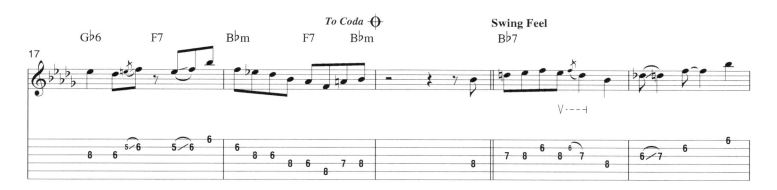

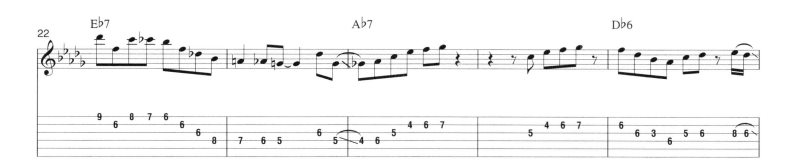

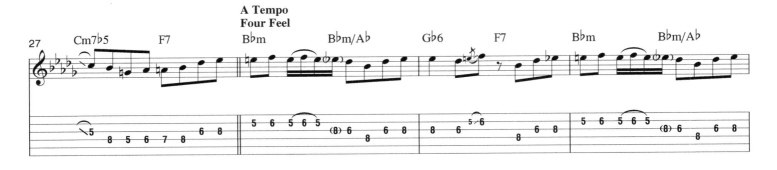

Figure 8—Guitar Solo, Recap and Coda

Kessel's guitar solo B C D is one of his finest early flights. It takes place over three choruses of the thirty-two-measure form and incorporates many lines and gestures borrowed from Charlie Christian and reinvented for this homage. Chief among these are the predominately rhythmic passages with overt syncopations, staccato phrasing, and repeated tones, the emphasis on the 6th degree in the minor mode throughout, bluesy string bends, groove riffs, and swinging single-note lines arranged in strings of eighth notes.

Unsurprisingly, there are numerous deliberate allusions to Charlie Christian's music, such as the licks in measures 1–2, 8–12, 20–21, 25–26, 28–29, 36–40, 41–44, 52–54, and elsewhere. Kessel even quotes the melody from "Till Tom Special," a primary piece from Christian's Benny Goodman period, outright in measures 45–47 and again in measures 65–67. Clearly linked to his idol's playing, Kessel's borrowings only reinforce the authentic mood of the tribute and never fall into hollow impersonations.

Kessel tempers his many references to Christian's swing era style with modern innovations from the bebop genre. Note the mix of bop and swing melody in measures 17–21, a swing riff punctuated by a Bird-inspired diminished arpeggio in measures 25–28, and bebop interval leaps, chromaticism, and enclosure figures in measures 76–78 and 80–84. Moreover, Kessel applies lines derived from the B♭ Harmonic Minor Scale for bop-oriented cadence melodies in measures 24, 56, and 88.

An elaborated recall of the tune's theme in measures 94–96 begins a transition back to the head. The arrangement of the sixteen-measure recap consists of the first two A sections, or the first half of the thirty-two-measure form. The coda grows out of the theme's final cadence, which is repeated three times as a tag. The final phrase is a series of chromatically rising minor-sixth chords—a paraphrase of a big-band figure reinterpreted in a combo setting.

Fig. 8

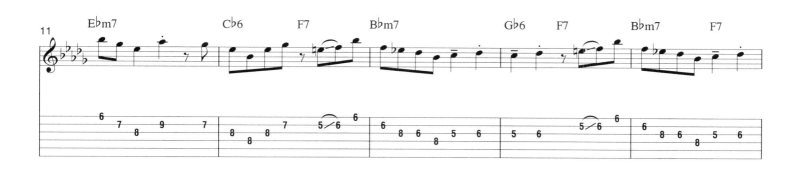

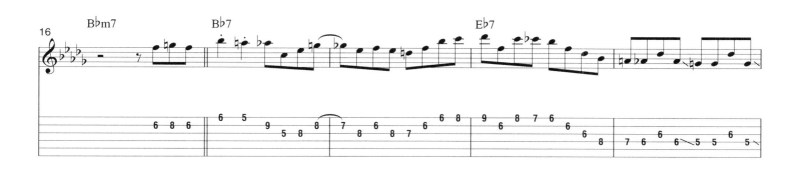

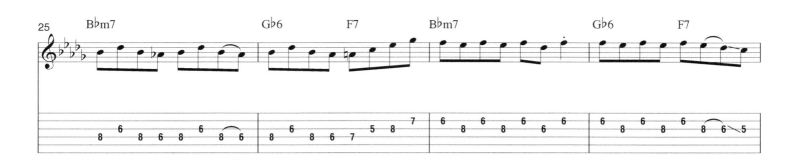

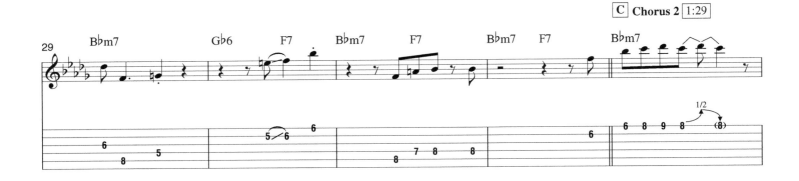

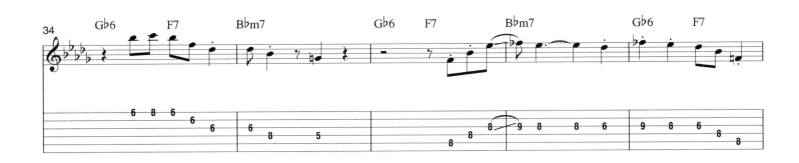

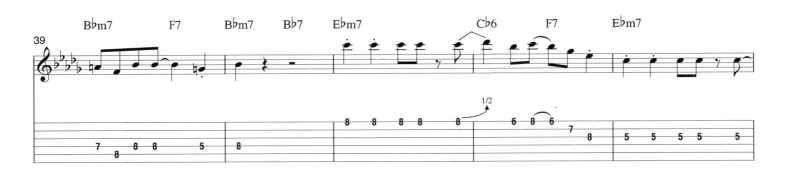

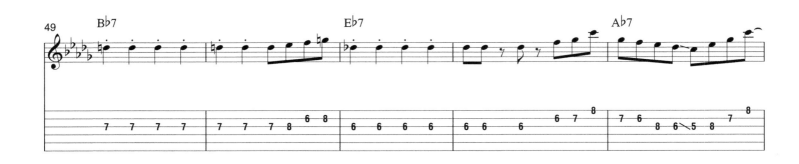

30

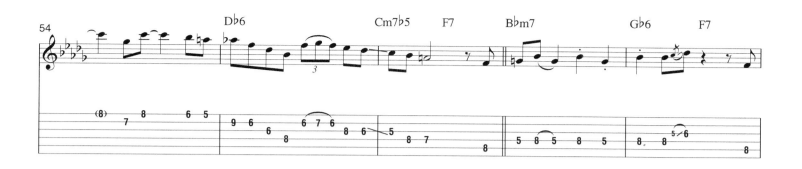

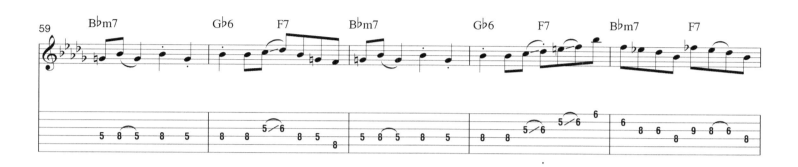

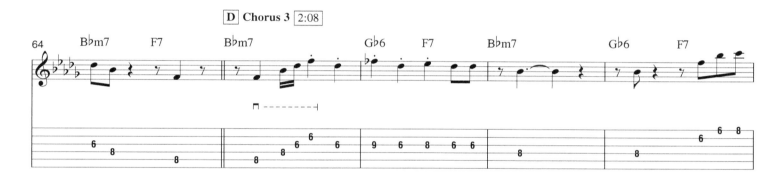

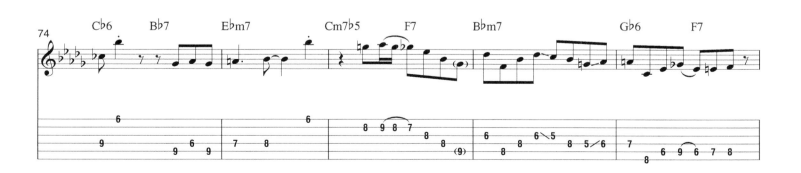

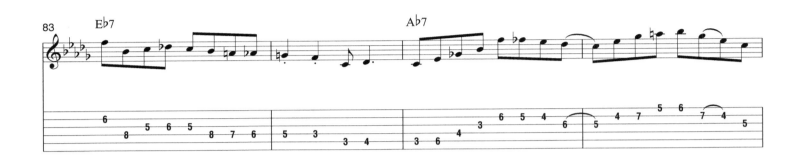

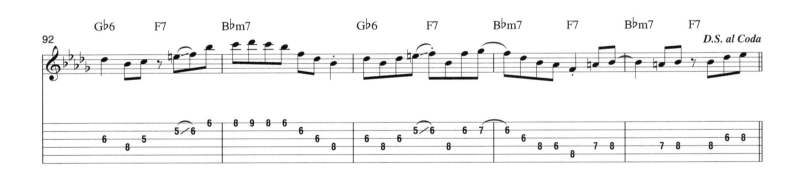

SPEAK LOW

from the Musical Production ONE TOUCH OF VENUS
(*Kessel Plays Standards: Barney Kessel, Volume 2*)
Words by Ogden Nash
Music by Kurt Weill

Figure 9—Intro and Head

Barney Kessel's sophomore release was appropriately titled *Barney Kessel Plays Standards*. As with his debut album, the tracks were collected from earlier sessions in 1954 and 1955. Though there was an emphasis in the set on classic standards from the likes of Duke Ellington, the Gershwins, and Rodgers and Hart, Kessel flexed his own compositional muscles and contributed two superb originals: "Barney's Blues" and "64 Bars on Wilshire." Joining Kessel in the sessions were Hampton Hawes or Claude Williamson (piano), Red Mitchell or Monty Budwig (bass), Bob Cooper (oboe and sax), and Chuck Thompson or the ubiquitous Shelly Manne (drums).

"Speak Low," a perennial favorite from Kurt Weill and Ogden Nash, was recorded on June 4, 1954, with Cooper, Williamson, Budwig, and Manne, and featured Kessel's penchant for thoughtful arranging and unusual instrumental combinations. Earlier, he was the first to use the flute as a solo voice in combo jazz. Here, he exploited the unique pairing of guitar and oboe to deliver the song's haunting theme. As a result, the decidedly modal melody, emphasizing the 9th of G minor (A), took on a bittersweet quality with the guitar/oboe timbre. Moreover, Kessel's arrangement posed the alternation of Latin and swing feels in the song's A sections, reserving a straight-ahead walking swing groove for the B section.

"Speak Low" is a large, uncommon fifty-six-measure song form: A(16)–A(16)–B(8)–A(16). Kessel's rendering of the theme B in the A sections is succinct and understated, as befits the terse melody statement played in unison with the oboe. Note the parallel harmony and its substitute-chord implications applied to the transitional line between verses in measures 17–18. In the B sections, Kessel takes the lead and plays a freer version of the melody, largely in swinging eighth-note rhythm.

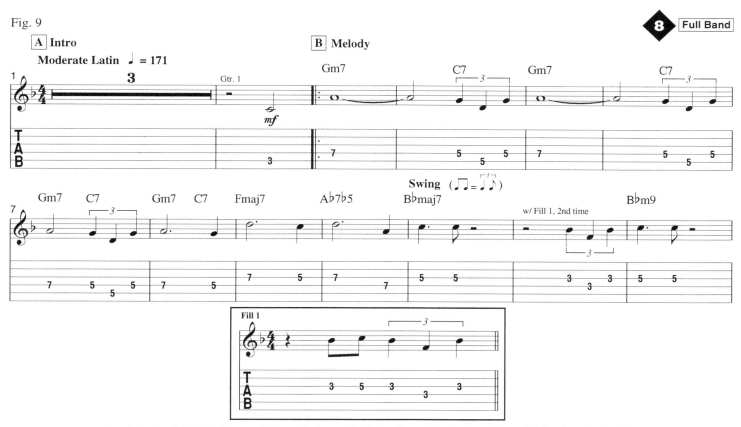

Figure 10—Solo and Recap

    Kessel's solo [C] takes place over the first forty measures of the song form (AAB). This is one of his most relaxed, concise, and melodious improvisations. He pursues riff-oriented ideas in measures 46–51, emphasizing the 9th tone (A) of the song's G minor melody. In measures 52–53, Kessel develops contrast with a rhythmic repeated-note figure. He converts a B♭ major-mode line laced with chromaticism to parallel minor (B♭m), a favorite tactic, in measures 54–57. Note the similar phrasing and rhythm. In measures 58–60, Kessel develops a sequential melody through the G7–Gm7 changes and concludes with a classic jazz phrase ending in F.

    Kessel switches gears in the second A section. He begins with a bluesy string-bending riff in measures 62–64, followed by a major-blues line in measures 65–67 phrased as a string of swung eight notes. He provides further contrast with a line from the bebop language in measures 68–70. Note the use of the F major hexatonic scale in measure 68, followed by an A diminished arpeggio as a substitute for A♭7 and the syncopated Bird-inspired phrase ending in B♭ in the two subsequent measures.

    Kessel plays idiomatic raked-picked arpeggios over B♭ minor in measure 72. Truly signature licks, these figures appear often in many forms, contexts, and variations in his improvisations. Here, they define a B♭m9 arpeggio in two octaves. Kessel pursues sequential riff-based patterns in the B section, measures 78–80, over Fm9 and D♭9. He wraps up his solo with major-mode hexatonic lines in E♭.

    Kessel returns to the song form with an abbreviated version of the head out, a final playing of the last A section with the original guitar/oboe orchestration. The arrangement closes with a quirky angular line in measures 85–86. Note the use of tonality-defying interval stacks made exclusively of tritones and 4ths. These eccentric "chords" are moved across the strings mathematically in a staggered fingering shape (frets 6, 7, and 8 on ascending three-string sets). This modernistic sound later found favor with post-bop, fusion, and even adventurous rock guitarists, but Kessel was most likely the first to exploit, and here showcase, the musical effect in mainstream jazz.

Fig. 10

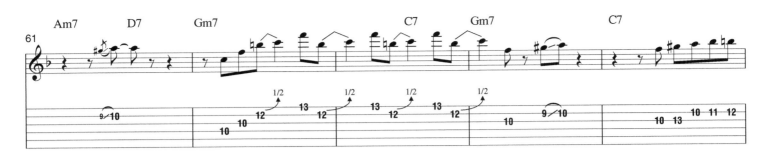

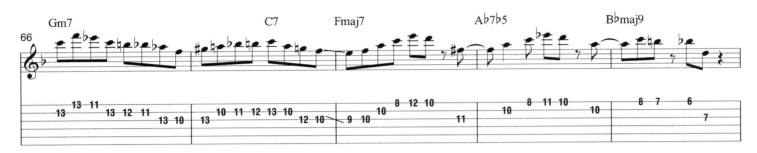

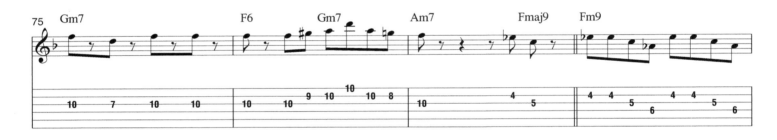

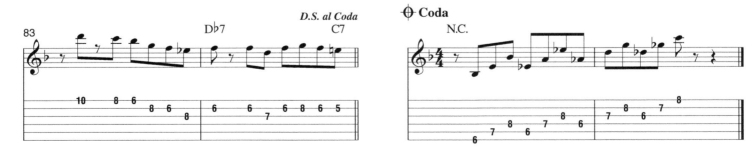

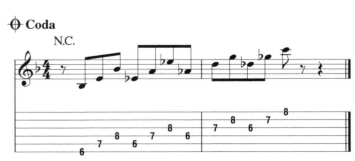

ON A SLOW BOAT TO CHINA

(*Kessel Plays Standards: Barney Kessel, Volume 2*)

By Frank Loesser

Figure 11—Head

"On a Slow Boat to China" received a rejuvenated jazz treatment by Kessel and company. Recorded on the same date and with the same players as "Speak Low," it was transformed from a campy pop song into a spirited bebop vehicle and stands as one of Kessel's career high points. Originally written in B♭, "On a Slow Boat to China" was performed by Kessel in E♭. It was given an appropriately straight-ahead arrangement with a tight rendering of the theme by guitar and sax and delivered at a moderately-fast swing tempo.

Like many jazz interpreters of standards, Kessel took liberties with the original melody line. In the head Ⓐ, he slightly but substantively rewrote the theme to stress characteristic jazz embellishments, syncopations, and more elaborate rhythmic phrasing. Kessel's refinements include bebop approach and enclosure figures in measures 4, 8, 20, and 24, chromatic passing tones in measures 7 and 23, and chromatic lower neighbor notes in measures 11 and 13. Moreover, he and saxophonist Bob Cooper play an attractive harmonized sequence in measures 15–16.

Fig. 11

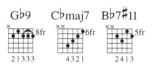

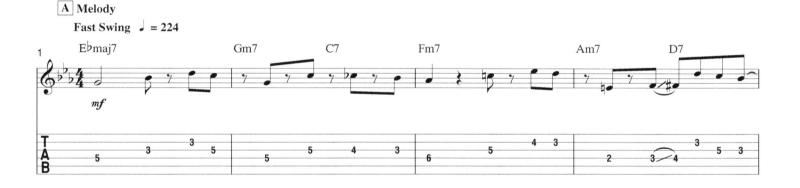

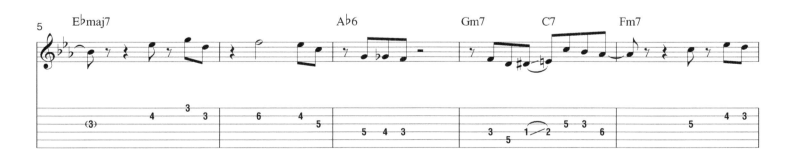

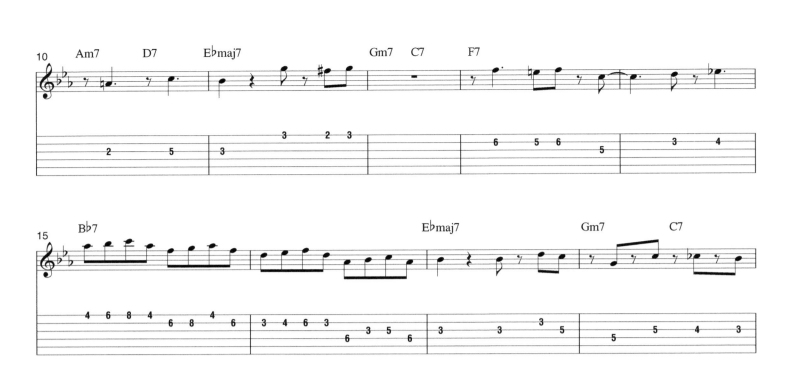

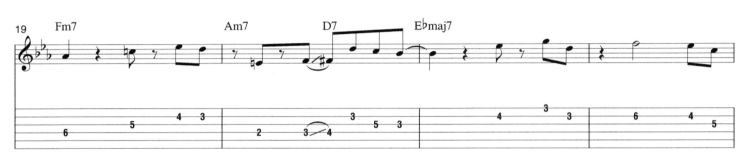

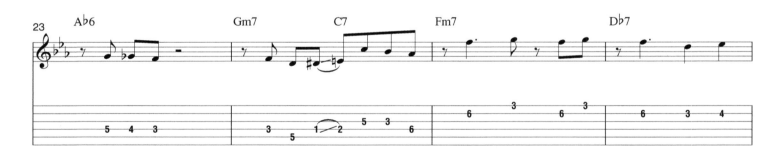

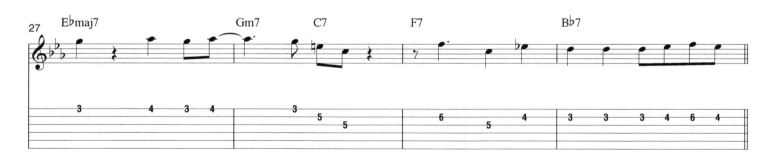

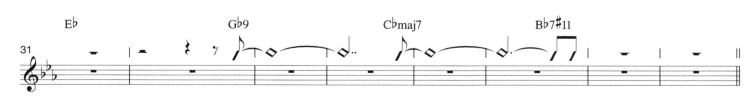

Figure 12—Guitar Solo and Recap

Kessel sets up his solo with an eight-measure interlude. He enters at the transition between choruses over E♭6–G♭7–C♭maj7–B♭7♯11 changes. A modern progression, similar to a bebop blues turnaround and the 3rds-related changes of John Coltrane, this type of pattern had been in the air since "Parker's Mood." Here, it serves as a bridge between the head and solo choruses. Note Kessel's use of a hexatonic scale as the source of melodies, in differing harmonic relationships, over E♭6 and G♭7 in measures 1–2 and 3–4. These are contrasted by a favorite major-mode bop cliché over C♭maj7 and a dissonant arpeggio riff over B♭7♯11. Check out the implicit E major (flatted 5th) chord outline stressed in the latter.

Kessel's swinging thirty-two-measure solo B begins in the bop vein with two melodious licks sequenced over Gm7–C7–Fm7 and Am7–D7–E♭maj7 in measures 10–13. Note similar chromatic approach figures and chord-related 6th leaps in the two phrases. Kessel momentarily suggests an augmented-chord sound in measure 14 with the chromatic motion to the C tone and plays an indispensable ii–V–i bebop lick for the passage into F minor in measures 15–17.

Two powerful bop melodies are found in the next phrase. Check out the zigzagging interval jumps in measure 19 and the imitated enclosure figure in measures 21–22. Kessel closes the first half of his solo with a rising stepwise line and voice-leading pattern over F7 and applies a variation of the famed "Honeysuckle Rose" lick in measures 23–24. Note the 4th relations in the phrase—Kessel plays a tonal version in B♭7 in measure 23 and answers with a similar figure in E♭ in measure 24.

Kessel's improvisations in the second half of the solo contain several thematic elements heard earlier. He revisits the idea of sequenced melodies and strong chord-related sounds with interval leaps in measures 25–28. This strikes the ear as an elaboration of his opening thoughts. Arpeggio outlines in measures 29–30 give way to melodically involved bop figures in measures 31–32 and a largely rhythmic episode in measures 33–35. In his closing thoughts, Kessel combines a chord-outlining bebop lick (measure 36) with a rhythmic phrase (measure 37) and a major-blues line (measures 38–39). Note the use of mixed major and minor 3rds (G and F♯ or G♭) in the latter as well as the prominent use of the 6th tone, C.

Kessel and Cooper restate the unison and harmonized theme C in measures 41–70. The interlude is recalled and varied to form a coda in measures 71–78. Kessel plays new improvisations in this section, including a major-blues line over E♭ in measures 71–72, a quick ascending scale run over G♭7 in measure 73, a chromatic bop pattern and arpeggio over C♭maj7 in measures 75–76, and a stepwise hexatonic melody in measure 77. His final phrase is a direct quote from the bebop language and is, in fact, a favorite Bird phrase ending.

Fig. 12

Guitar entrance 1:50

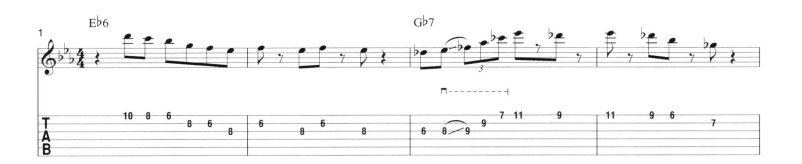

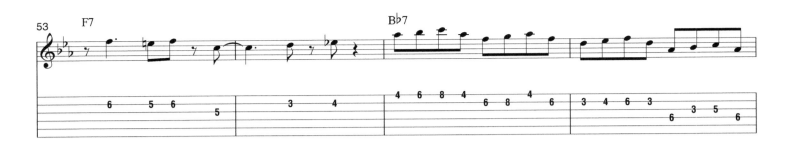

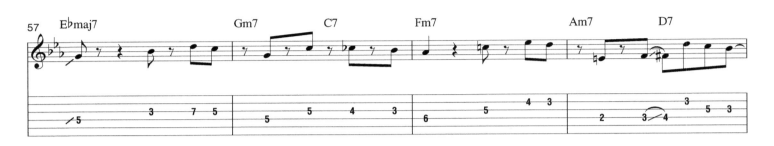

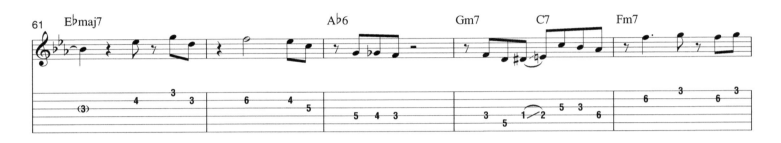

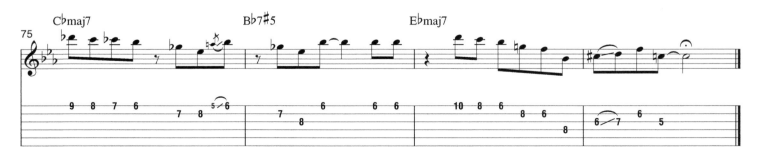

BARNEY'S BLUES
(*Kessel Plays Standards: Barney Kessel, Volume 2*)
By Barney Kessel

Figure 13—Intro and Head

Every great Barney Kessel album contains a healthy measure of the blues. *Kessel Plays Standards* is no exception. On this collection, Kessel contributed a noteworthy original, simply titled "Barney's Blues," which reconciles his straight blues and slick bop inclinations. The track was recorded on July 1, 1954, with his then-core group of Bob Cooper, Claude Williamson, Monty Budwig, and Shelly Manne.

"Barney's Blues" comes off like a sequel to his previous "Easy Like." Like the earlier piece, it's in C and in the head marries a country-like fingerstyle approach to modern bop-oriented chord changes. This was purportedly Kessel's first attempt to record a tune with only the fingers, a concept based on simultaneously stating the simple blues melody with a contrapuntal walking bass line.

Kessel begins the proceedings with a pianistic blues riff in the intro [A]. This is played as a dialoguing duet with guitar and drums. Note the slurred articulation, pedal tones, and shifted rhythm in Kessel's two opening phrases. These are separated and offset by rhythmically defining drum fills.

In the head [B] Kessel expands the orchestration to include the bass—a brief and prescient example of his guitar-bass-drums trio texture. His initial playing of the theme in the is contrapuntal, comprised of a simple descending blues melody (fixed) accompanied by a harmonically active, ascending counter melody (flexible) in the bass register. During the course of the tune's 12-bar form, he makes purposeful variations to the bass line, modifying it to reflect the changing harmony. The main theme is punctuated by short rising chord phrases from the tonic major mode (Cmaj7–Dm7–Em7) in measures 12 and 16, and strong cadential progressions, C13sus4–C7♯5 to F in measures 12–13, Em11–A7♯5 to Dm7 in measures 16–18, and Dm11–D♭9 to C7 in measures 20–22.

In the second time through the head, Kessel modifies his theme, converting it to a single-note line in measures 21–31. Here, it is played as a unison melody with Cooper's oboe—an unusual orchestral choice for a blues tune and typical of Kessel's adventurous arranging inclinations. Also notable in the arrangement is the entrance of the piano at the second [B] section, which supplies support in the form of a doubled bass line and chord accompaniment in short, accented figures with Kessel and enlarges the instrumental forces to a quintet texture.

Fig. 13

Figure 14—Guitar Solo and Recap

Kessel enters the arrangement as a soloist at 1:46 with a four-bar chordal interlude of descending ii–V patterns. These contain prominent 9th and 11th color tones. They move in whole-step increments following a *cycle-of-fourths* progression from Gm7 to G7: Gm7 (11)–C7, Fm7 (11)–Bb7, and Ebm7 (11)–Ab13–G13.

Kessel begins his two-chorus solo with a bluesy string-bending sequence in measures 4–7. The overall sound reflects the C blues scale (C–Eb–F–Gb–G–Bb) and his Oklahoma country-blues roots. Note the use of added 6th and 9th tones in the line. Kessel pursues riff-based sounds in measures 8–10 over F7 and concludes with a mixed minor and major blues melody. Down-home Oklahoma twang gives way to uptown bebop in measures 13–14, where he plays a longer and more complex double-timed line laced with chromaticism over the ii–V change. Kessel concludes his first chorus in a blues vein with a rhythmically charged pentatonic scale sequence, like a compressed version of his opening phrase.

Kessel changes strategies for his second chorus D, turning to block chords in place of single-note textures and pursuing an approach akin to the "shout choruses" of the big-band genre. His solo is structured in three discrete phrases defining the three-part blues form. Kessel applies his favorite *quartal* voicings (4th intervals), chromaticism, and parallel motion to color the blues line in measures 17–19. His cadence in measure 20 exploits an often-used triad pattern to harmonize the F–E♭–C pentatonic melody. Kessel plays a similar blues line harmonized in parallel dominant ninth chords over F7 in measures 21–22 and returns to quartal voicings and a variation of his cadential figure in measures 23–24. The final blues phrase finds Kessel forming a progression of triads, parallel 13th chords, and quartal sonorities.

Kessel recalls the first 12 bars of the head, in its original contrapuntal form with guitar-bass-drums trio instrumentation, at E. His final cadence features a favorite thumb-fretted voicing of a complex altered chord, D♭9♯11/A♭, and a partial thirteenth chord, C13/B♭. Note the thumb fretting across the sixth and fifth strings in the D♭9♯11 chord. This is a signature Kessel technique ubiquitous in his playing.

Fig. 14

45

*T = Thumb on 6th string

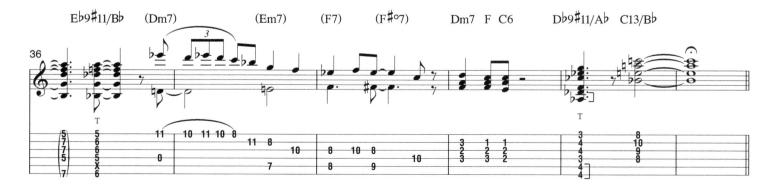

64 BARS ON WILSHIRE

(*Kessel Plays Standards: Barney Kessel, Volume 2*)

By Barney Kessel

Figure 15—Intro and Head

The tune "64 Bars on Wilshire" is a sophisticated Kessel jazz original also recorded on July 1, 1954, with the Cooper/Williamson/Budwig/Manne lineup. A more intricate long form distinguishes the A–B–C–B tune: A(16)–B(16)–C(16)–B(16)—sixty-four-measures instead of the usual thirty-two-measure form of most standard songs. The arrangement of the head B features an unusual treatment of the melody during A and B sections, suggested by Manne, in which Kessel and Cooper play the first thirty-two-measures of theme without a defined rhythm background. This imparts an abstract feeling to the first half of the sixty-four-measure form and provides an intriguing contrast to Kessel's rhythmic eight-measure chordal intro A, accompanied only by Manne and his fills, and the full band entrance at measure 36.

Kessel's complex theme B in the A and B sections is a zigzagging, rhythmically-charged bop line outlining the tune's modulatory chord changes. Note the characteristic angular interval leaps to altered chord tones and extensions (as in the harmonically- related jumps from C down to E♭ in measure 9 and C up to B in measure 13), chromaticism, syncopation, and bebopping rhythmic phrasing.

The full ensemble entrance at the bridge C (0:34) finds Kessel and Cooper abandoning the tight unison delivery of the melody. Kessel plays ostinato riff figures through the changes in measures 36–41 over Cooper's simple counterpoint. He maintains the riff approach over the changes in measures 44–45 and addresses the cadences in measures 42–43 and 46–47 with similar bop phrase endings, emphasizing 6th tones in G and A♭. Kessel's last two statements are strong but unresolved ii–V phrases that lead to the recall of the main theme (B section) and solos.

Figure 16—Guitar Solo and Recap

Kessel begins his solo ⬜D with rhythmic motives. He plays a simple sequential melody of few notes distinguished by syncopation and staccato phrasing over the Am7♭5–D7–Bm7♭5–E7 changes in measures 1–4. His longer bop lines in measures 5–8 contrast and complement these sounds nicely. Note the approach to the Am7–D7–G changes in strings of eighth notes with characteristic chromatic passing tones and melodic leaps, bebop enclosure figures, and extended arpeggios. A similar conception informs the two ensuing lines in measures 9–12 (F♯m7–B7–E) and 13–15 (Em7–A7–Am7). The former phrase contains a favorite cadential line over F♯m7–B7.

Rake picking is applied to the imitative lines in measures 17–22. Kessel expands a short chromatic fragment in measures 25–26, uniting Am7 and Cm7 chords on different scale levels. The fragment appears again briefly to begin his phrase in measure 29.

A rhythmic motive is developed over Fm7–B♭7–E♭maj7 in measures 33–36. By contrast, bebop chromaticism and swinging eighth-note strings characterize the improvisations over Am7–D7–Gmaj7. Note the use of A♭ sounds over Am7–D7 in the line; this exemplifies typical *tritone substitution* of the bop vernacular.

Kessel's rake picking technique appears again in the quick slurred arpeggio melodies in measures 41–43 and pervades a trademark phrase in measures 49–52. Here, Kessel applies upstrokes to minor arpeggio figures arranged in a sequential pattern over Am7♭5–D7–Bm7♭5–E7. Note the characteristic bop tonal relationships: Cm9 over Am7♭5, E♭m9 over D7, Dm9 over Bm7♭5, and Fm9 over E7.

In a tight thematic wrap-up, Kessel alludes to and develops the chromatic fragment of measures 25–26 through Cm7–B♭maj7–B♭° changes in measures 58–60. Kessel closes his solo in a soulful vein with an overt minor pentatonic line complete with string bends over G major in measures 62–64.

Kessel rejoins the arrangement at the bridge ⬜E. He restates the ostinato figures heard earlier over Cooper's counter melody in measures 65–70 and 73–74 and elaborates slightly on material over Gmaj7–G6 in measures 71–72 and A♭maj7 in measure 75. New improvisations are added to the bridge in measures 76–80. Note the use of riff-oriented melodies over A♭maj7–A♭6 and F♯m7–B7, the use of C minor sounds on Am7♭5, and the unison figure on D7.

Kessel and company take the tune out with a repeat of the final B section. The closing line in the coda is a quick two-octave arpeggio run, which defines a fast ii–V–I progression (Am7–D7–G) in G.

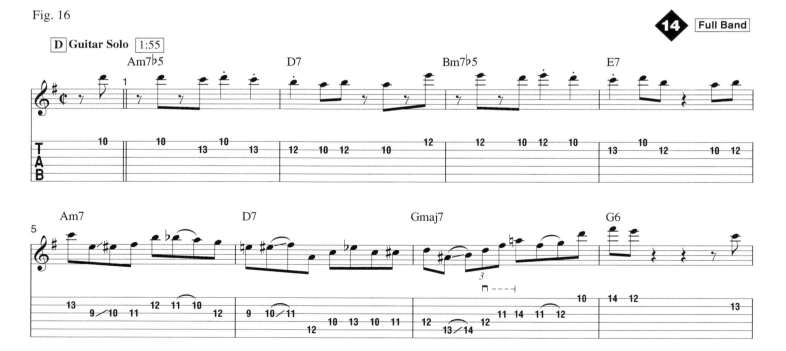

Fig. 16

 ... (placed above)

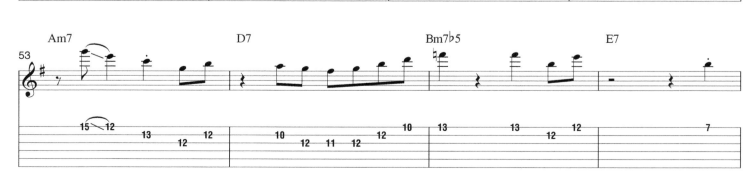

* Hammer-on 3rd string
without picking

BEGIN THE BLUES

(*To Swing or Not to Swing: Barney Kessel, Volume 3*)

By Barney Kessel

Figure 17—Intro and Head

Barney Kessel followed *Plays Standards* with a third impressive offering: the playfully titled *To Swing or Not to Swing (Volume 3)*, a proposition the guitarist addressed on his guitar in no uncertain musical terms. Astute players and savvy listeners across genres and generations have long acknowledged the material on Kessel's three-album debut series as containing the most definitive and influential performances of his classic years. Joining Kessel in the two sessions of 1955 that comprised the third album were Harry "Sweets" Edison (trumpet), George Auld or Bill Perkins (sax), Jimmy Rowles (piano), Al Hendrickson (rhythm guitar), Red Mitchell (bass), and Shelly Manne or Irv Cottler (drums).

The opening track "Begin the Blues" was recorded on July 26, 1955, as a quartet with Kessel, Rowles, Mitchell, and Cottler and stands as a testament of his swinging blues-based guitar style. This Kessel original is a 12-bar blues tune in B♭ sporting a no-frills combo arrangement and a quirky three-part theme in the head [A]. The first part is a space-conscious line with an angular wide-interval melody and repeated notes in measures 1–3. The second is a call-and-response phrase that outlines E♭7 and B♭7 changes in measures 4–7. The third is a variation of the first phrase played over Cm7–F7 changes in measures 9–10. The entire head statement is punctuated by rests, which set the phrases apart and drive home the three-part structure.

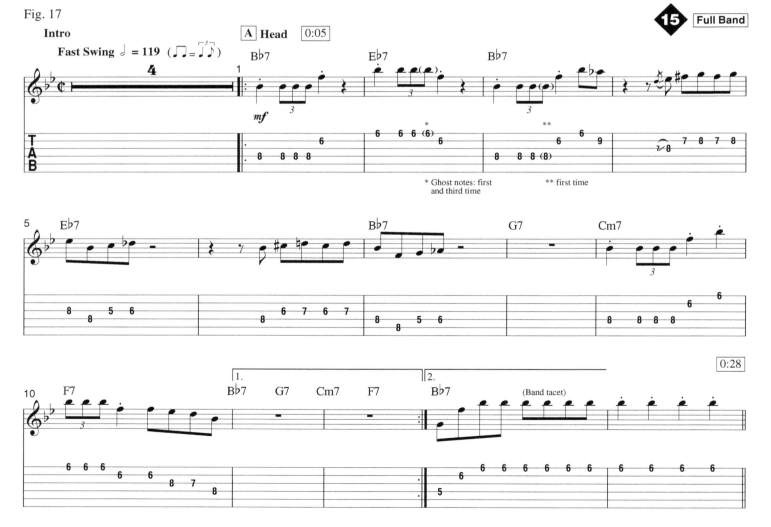

Figure 18—Guitar Solo

Kessel takes the first solo immediately after the twenty-four-measure head. This improvisation is one of the longest flights of his early years: eight inventive choruses of 12-bar blues, B through I, in B♭. Each chorus contains a wealth of signature licks.

1. B Kessel plays rhythmic ideas in his pickup phrase (second ending of the head) and the first measure. The deliberate staccato articulation of repeated notes is an identi- fier of his style. Kessel quickly establishes the *major/minor polarity* of the blues in measures 2–4, which prevails throughout the solos. Note the pivotal G and D♭ tones in the phrase.

2. C Kessel cultivates a swing-oriented riff to begin his second chorus. The repetition of the core pattern results in a funky *call-and-response* phrase in measures 13–16. His cadential line in measures 21–23 contains bebop chromaticism, upper-partial melodies mixed with blues sounds, and a swing-genre phrase ending.

3. D Kessel milks a momentum-gathering riff in measures 25–28 over B♭ and E♭7. He plays a gradual string bend in measures 32–33, setting the mood for coming blues-guitar elaborations.

4. E Kessel develops short repeated rhythmic riffs and syncopation in measures 37–41. Charlie Christian and bop references are discernable in measures 44–45. Note the reference to the "Seven Come Eleven" melody at the phrase ending.

5. F String bending distinguishes Kessel's fifth chorus. Note his bends into the A♭ blue note in two sections, measures 49–50 and 53–54. Together these form a longer call-and-response phrase.

6. G Kessel subjects riff figures to shifted and compressed rhythm in measures 61–63. He adds a harmonically active *contrary-motion* dyad figure to the phrase as a cadential closing idea.

7. H Kessel plays swing-oriented riffs that would not be out of place in a fifties rock 'n' roll song in measures 73–74. He leans on A♭, the "money note" of the blues, in measure 76. He paraphrases Bird in the bop approach figure of measures 80–81; this phrase comes off like a modified fragment of "Billie's Bounce."

8. I Kessel exploits string-bending and blues scale licks in measures 85–88 and a swinging blues riff in measures 89–90. Note the prominence of G and D♭ tones in the latter. His turnaround lick in measures 95–97 combines arpeggio sounds (G–B♭–D–F) with an enclosure figure (F–E–D–E♭) and a leading-tone (B♭–A–B♭) closing melody.

Fig. 18

15 **Full Band**
cont.

B Guitar Solo: Chorus 1

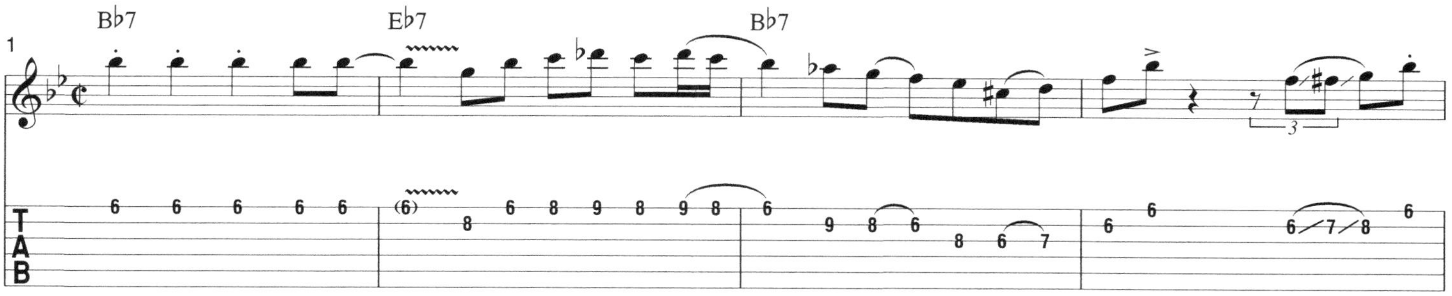

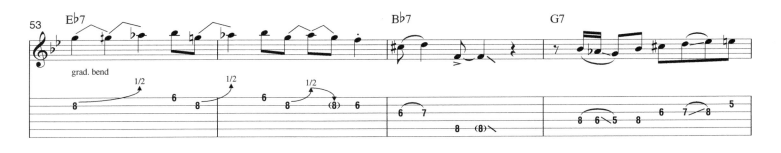

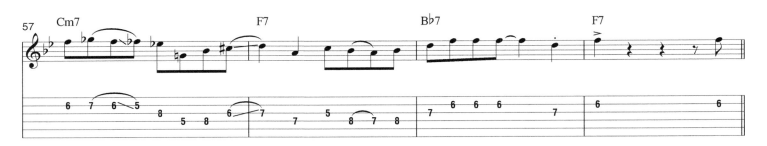

G Chorus 6

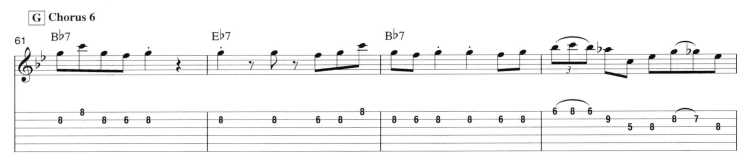

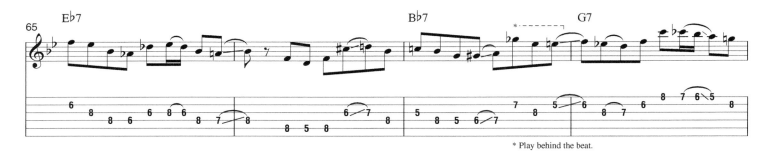

* Play behind the beat.

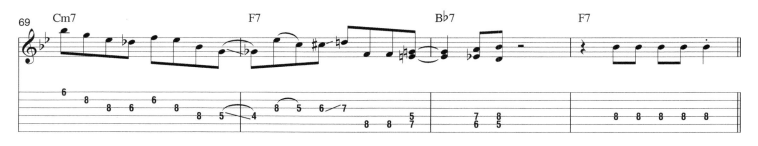

H Chorus 7

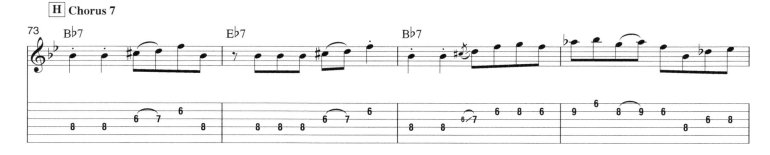

I **Chorus 8**

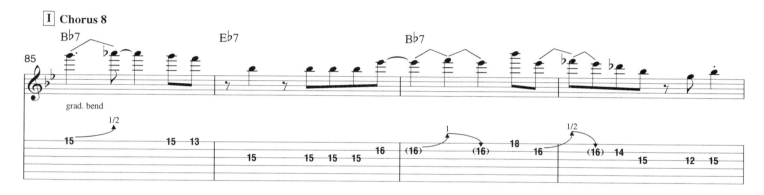

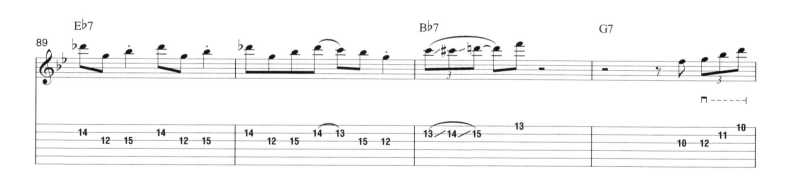

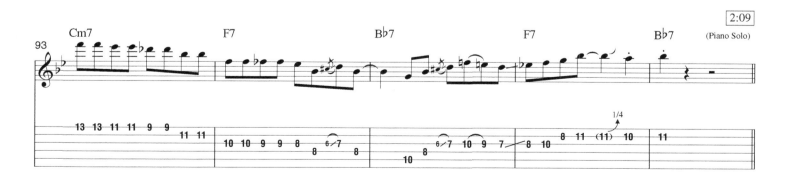

Figure 19—Trading Fours, Guitar Solo 2 and Recap

Kessel re-enters the arrangement at 2:45 after the piano solo and pursues a *trading-fours* interlude, passing four-measure phrases back and forth with Rowles. This is a traditional procedure in blowing jazz and is often found in impromptu blues performances. Here, Kessel plays concise melodies, which contrastingly take the lead, overlap, comment on, and play off the pianist's licks. The twenty-four-measure trading section J leads to a second guitar solo of three choruses K, L, and M.

Kessel's trading phrases include a rhythmically-charged repeated-note line in measures 1–3, a longer and more complex bop phrase replete with his raked arpeggio figures in measures 7–11, and imitative swing riffs punctuated by octave bursts in measures 15–18. Kessel expands his final trading phrase of measures 25–29 into a bop-inflected pickup line to launch his second guitar solo.

Kessel's second solo reprises many sounds and ideas from his first solo. In the first chorus K he begins with staccato repeated notes, swing-oriented riffs, and major-blues melody, emphasizing the pivotal 6th tone in measures 30–33. His call-and-response lines combine minor and major blues melody in measures 34–37 and are endowed with unmistakable harmonic allusions, notably the tones E (suggesting an implied E diminished passing chord) and G (the tonic of G7). The closing phrase contains bebop chromaticism, and chord outlining of Cm9, and a swing-based ending lick.

Kessel pursues rhythmic riffs and phrasing at length in his second chorus L. Note the prominent syncopation, staccato punctuation of quarter notes, and strategic use of space (rests). Kessel's phrases are short, simple melodically, and imitative as befits the funkier side of the blues.

Kessel's final chorus M ups the funky blues intensity with two extended string-bending phrases in measures 54–61. His first is a riff of unison bends (a staple of guitar blues) arranged in short repetitive patterns, shifted rhythmically. His second is a descending two-and-a-half-octave melody in which the underlying blues scale is decorated with primarily half-step bends. Kessel's final thoughts unabashedly acknowledge the swing genre with two Charlie Christian-inspired blues licks.

Kessel recapitulates his blues head with slight variations in N. He concludes the tune with a characteristic mixed-mode blues melody in measure 78. Note the straight descending stepwise motion, pull-offs, and minor-pentatonic structure expanded with 6th and 9th tones. While many will be tempted to label this as Dorian, the intent is completely different; essentially it is the colorizing of a simple pentatonic blues line. Kessel tags on a two-chord cadence pattern in measure 79. Note the similarly shaped forms and chromatic motion that produce the F7–B♭7♭5 progression.

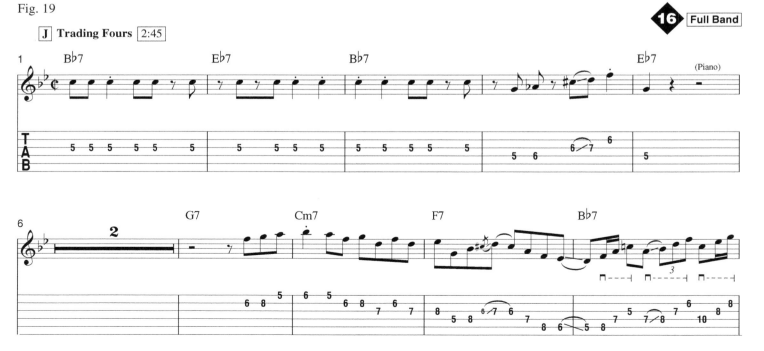

Fig. 19

J **Trading Fours** 2:45

16 Full Band

* Emphasize lower note of octave.

K **Guitar Solo 2 : Chorus 1** 3:17

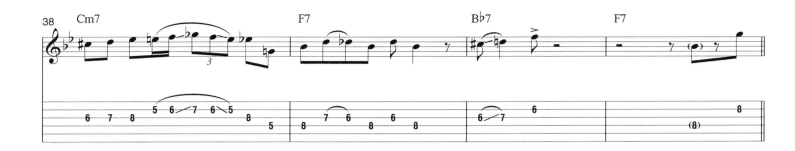

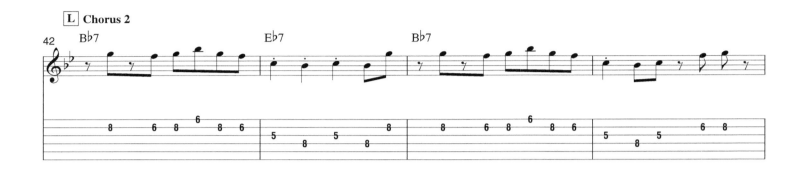

L Chorus 2

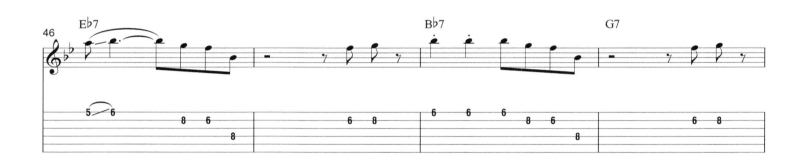

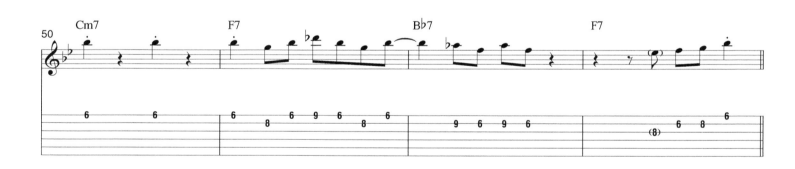

M Chorus 3

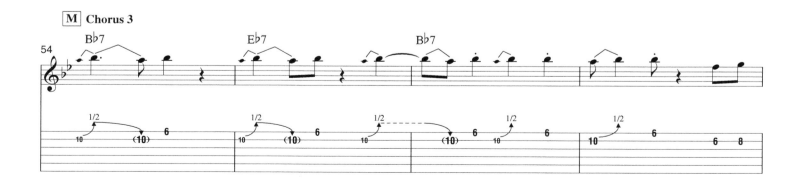

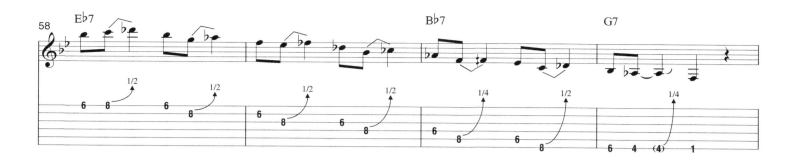

N **Head out** 3:59

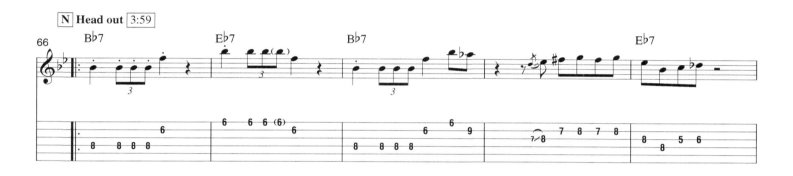

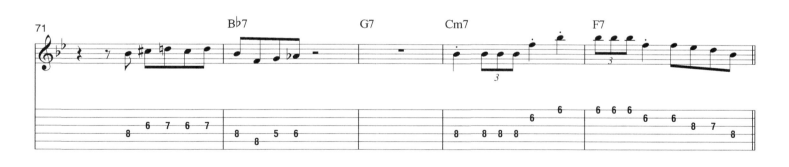

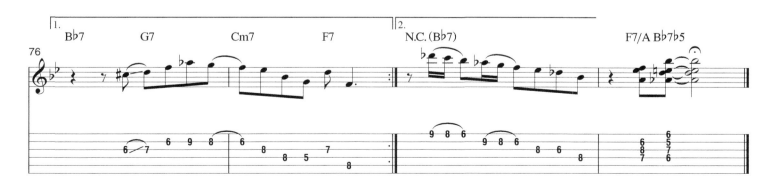

INDIANA (BACK HOME AGAIN IN INDIANA)

(To Swing or Not to Swing: Barney Kessel, Volume 3)

Words by Ballard MacDonald
Music by James Hanley

Figure 20—Intro and Head

"Indiana" is the immortal oldie from 1917 that inspired Charlie Parker to write his famed contrafact "Donna Lee." A favorite set of changes among bebop players, the original tune was largely ignored by modern jazz musicians after Bird's innovations. However, Kessel and company restored its relevance with a spirited rendition blending the historic schools of classic jazz, Dixieland, swing, and bebop. There are unmistakable hints of Dixieland jazz in the polyphonic New Orleans-style horn figures, while Kessel's playing reflects modernity and the fluent sax-like phrasing of swing and bop. "Indiana" was recorded on July 26, 1955, with Jimmy Rowles, Red Mitchell, Harry "Sweets" Edison, George Auld (sax), and Irv Cottler (drums). Kessel takes the tune at a fast cut-time tempo. Following Bird's lead and bop conventions, he largely adheres to the standard changes but transposes the original key of G major to A♭.

The arrangement begins with Kessel's brief unaccompanied guitar intro A in single notes. A familiar jazz convention—think Dexter Gordon's "Smile" or John Coltrane's "Countdown"—the practice has the powerful musical effect of explicitly showcasing the primary soloist at the outset. Here, Kessel outlines an implied A♭–A°–B♭m–B°–Fm7–B♭m7–E♭7–A♭ progression with a sequential, harmonically-defining line, largely in eighth notes. Note the idiomatic bop extension over B diminished in measure 2; here, Kessel plays a triadic melody (G major) derived from the underlying diminished scale. This modern sound, and the unmistakable arpeggio/enclosure figures in measure 3, underscore Kessel's fluency with the evolving bebop language.

Kessel states the thirty-two-measure head B with slight embellishments in measures 5–36, much as he had in an earlier reappraised oldie, "On a Slow Boat to China." However, here he tackles the theme as a freer guitar statement rather than a strict ensemble line. Kessel makes many rhythmic variations, adds connective fills and bop figures, and modernizes the harmony at crucial points in the arrangement. Note the syncopation in measures 5 and 34–36, stepwise runs in measures 8 and 24, bop phrase endings in measures 7, 11, 23, and 27, a slurred chromatic passing-tone fill in measure 12, the cadential figure in measures 19–20, riff patterns in measures 21–22, and extended arpeggios in measures 28–29 and 32. The latter is a repurposed version of his opening B diminished lick applied to A♭ diminished, a symmetrical inversion of the same chord. This thinking reveals Kessel's modern conception at work.

Fig. 20

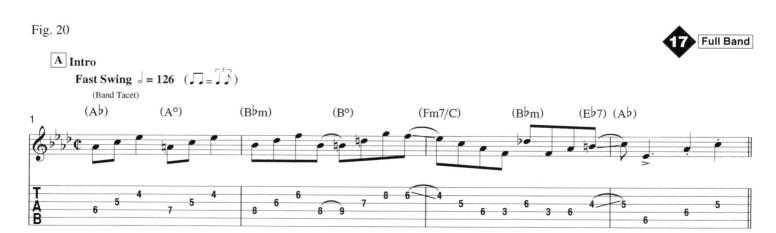

Figure 21—Guitar Solo 1

Kessel takes one solo chorus over the song form at 0:34 C. He begins in the low register with a swinging phrase marked by repetition, rhythmic figures, and riff patterns. In measures 17–20, Kessel states a surprising angular line of widely spaced arpeggios Note the 10th intervals over Ab–F7 and the raked shapes over Bb7. The latter are characteristic Kessel components, made of mixed augmented and major sounds articulated with his sweep-picking style.

The intricate F minor bop line in measures 21–23 is a direct paraphrase of horn players like Bird, Brownie, and Dizzy, and comes off like a harbinger of similar minor-mode patterns in modern guitarists like Wes Montgomery, Pat Martino, and George Benson. Note the bebop enclosure figures characteristically left and approached by interval jumps and the disguised chromatic passing-tone line at the phrase ending. Kessel plays an intervallic melody exploiting 6th leaps in measures 25–28 and concludes with a sequential hexatonic phrase in measures 29–31. His final line is a favorite ii–V–I pattern and acts as a concise "hand-over" to Edison for his trumpet solo.

Fig. 21

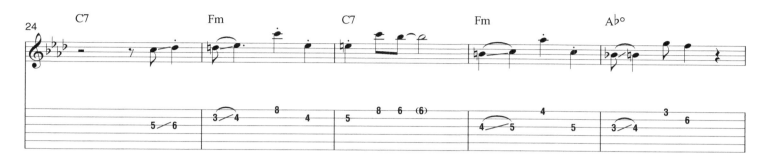

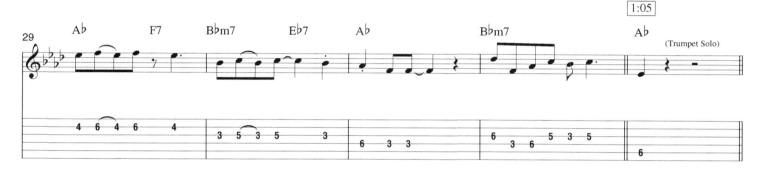

Figure 22—Guitar Solo 2 and Outro

Kessel's second solo D is purposely shorter and leads directly to a stop-time interlude and the tune's ending. He improvises over the first half of the form in measures 1–16 and then extemporizes around the basic theme in measures 17–24. As in his first solo, Kessel mixes primarily rhythmic phrases, like those in measures 1–4, with riffs (measures 9–11) bebop figures (measures 11–14), and a strong cadential pattern (measures 15–16).

Kessel embellishes the melody with rhythmic variations, fills, and a change in register in measures 17–24. He plays through the ensemble stop-time interlude with a strong bop line in measures 25–28. Note the final recall of his thematic diminished scale lick in measure 28, there played as raked figure. Kessel's final thoughts allude to his roots with a bluesy descending string-bending sequence during the band tacet. Check out his use of half-step bends to decorate the largely stepwise line.

Fig. 22

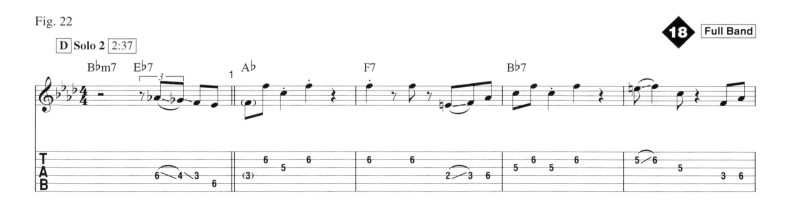

CONTEMPORARY BLUES

(*To Swing or Not To Swing: Barney Kessel, Volume 3*)

By Barney Kessel

Figure 23—Intro and Head

"Contemporary Blues" is definitive blues—Kessel style. With this track, the composer achieved an ideal balance of sophisticated harmonic elements (in the head) and straight-ahead blues improvisation (in solos). Aiding Kessel in that pursuit were the core personnel: Jimmy Rowles (piano), Red Mitchell (bass), and Shelly Manne (drums), augmented by Harry "Sweets" Edison (trumpet), Bill Perkins (tenor sax), and Al Hendrickson (rhythm guitar). The session took place in Los Angeles on March 28, 1955.

The intro A is made of two brief chord phrases, which are closely related to the main theme. Here, Kessel utilizes the compositional idea of foreshadowing by presenting elements of the theme in abbreviated form (two bars). Note the *pedal point* concept at work in measures 1–2 and 5–6. Kessel maintains Eb (the *pedal tone*) as the top voice of every chord in the chromatically-bound progressions: Bbm11–Eb7–Abmaj7–Abm7–Abm6–Gb13 and Am7b5–Abm7–Abm6–Gb13–F7–Emaj7, respectively. Each chord phrase is answered by a short bass break. At no point in the intro is the expected tonic chord, Eb, established or even stated.

In the head B, Kessel expounds on elements from the intro, most notably similar chord colors and pedal point. These longer phrases (four bars) are arranged and developed within in the traditional three-part structure of 12-bar blues. The first phrase comes off like a deceptive ii–V–I progression in Ab (measures 9–10) before briefly establishing Eb in measure 11. Note the use of similar Bbm11 and Eb7 voicings and pedal point, enlarged with a Gb–F melody. The idea of inserting this melody is maintained throughout the first two phrases.

The second phrase begins on the IV chord, Ab—a normal convention of the blues—before returning to Eb. The third and final phrase of the 12-bar form is a contrasting figure of ascending chords given a specific textural/rhythmic treatment. Note the repeated pattern of bass note and two upper chord partials for Fm7, Gm7#5, Ab6, and A°7. Furthermore, note the ubiquitous Eb pedal point in the top voice of every chord and the *three-against-four* rhythmic phrasing of the progression. Also noteworthy is the Emaj7 substitution for Bb11 in the final cadence of measure 18. The *Neapolitan* effect of approaching the tonic blues chord Eb from a half step above, and exploiting the Eb pedal tone to join the two, imparts a sophisticated and uncommon touch to the changes, typical of Kessel's sense of modern harmony.

The third phrase in measures 29–30 remains the same and functions as a strong transition to the band-tacet break launching Kessel's guitar solo.

Fig. 23

A Intro

Moderate Swing ♩ = 165

19 Full Band

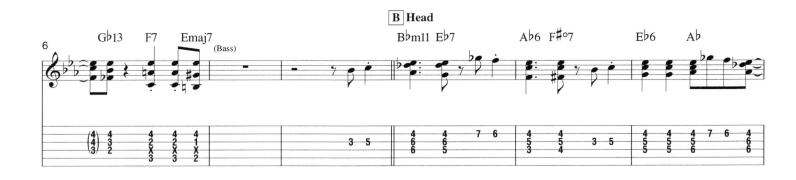

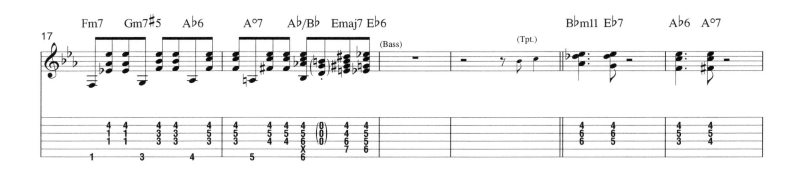

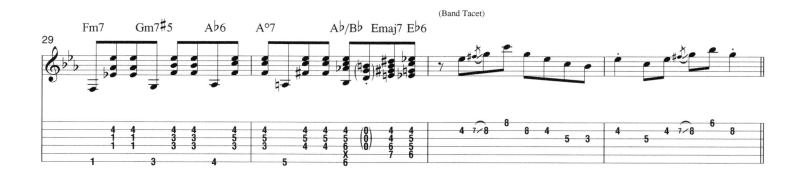

Figure 24—Guitar Solo

Kessel takes two choruses of 12-bar blues in E♭ for his solo. He begins with a pentatonic pickup line in the break, emphasizing C, the pivotal 6th tone of swing music. Swing and bop ideas are combined in his first chorus C, and he closes with a major pentatonic line conveying the sweeter side of the blues in measures 10–12.

In the opening of his second chorus D, Kessel doles out bluesy funk and musical contrast. He plays a pianistic double-stop riff in measures 12–14. In this phrase, he poses the E♭ blues scale and its piquant tensions under an E♭ pedal tone. Note his soulful two-against-three rhythmic phrasing, emphasized tritone, and slurs into the ♭5th blue note in measure 13.

Kessel wraps up the progression with a descending sequence exploiting perfect 4th intervals in measures 19–20, a suitable contemporary sound that adds further contrast to his solo. Kessel's final thoughts in measures 23–24 revert to the major pentatonic sounds heard at the outset.

Fig. 24

*Play behind the beat.

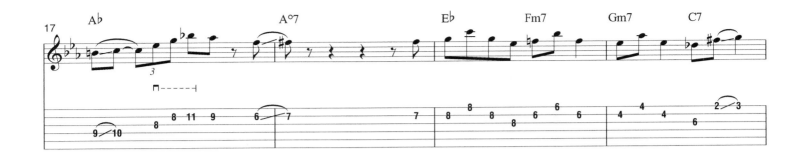

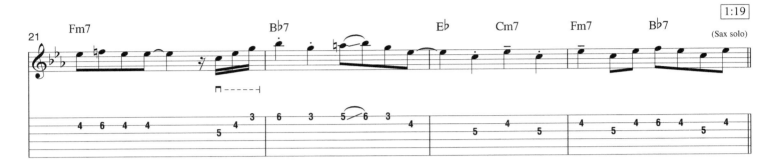

Figure 25—Interlude 1

Kessel and company lock into a swinging unison riff over the 12-bar form in the first interlude E at 2:25. This riff is a two-measure figure exploiting the major/minor polarity of blues. It lends further contrast and acts as a trading device for Mitchell's solo bass breaks. Note Kessel's connecting pattern outlining the A♭6–A°7–E♭6 progression with simple dyads in measures 2, 5, and 8. In the second chorus of the interlude, Mitchell's previous solo spaces are used to state a longer ensemble line, which grows organically out of the two-bar riff. Note the emphasized dissonance in crucial cadence spots: E♭7♯9 in measure 13 and C7♯9 in measure 17.

Fig. 25

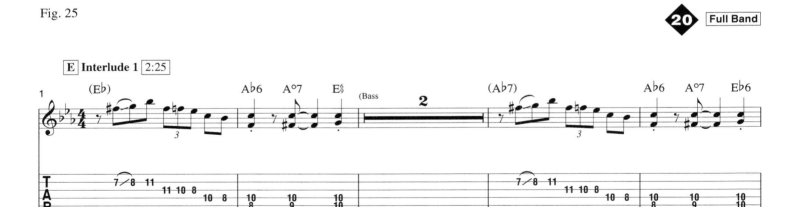

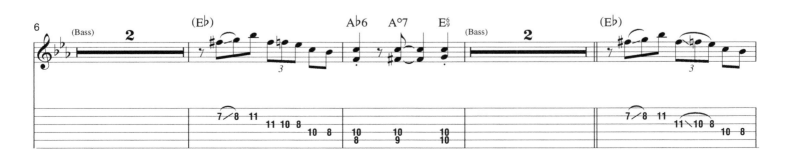

Figure 26—Interlude 2 and Recap

The second interlude ⬚F⬚ is an eight-measure section, which has a mysterious, harmonically vague quality—more related to contemporary classical guitar than the blues. Kessel's chord-melody style is the focal point here. He maintains an upper B♭ pedal tone while superimposing a progression of descending major-3rd dyads below. The voice leading is purely chromatic throughout. A similar parallel pattern is played in two octaves: first, the upper register in the pickup and measures 1–3 and then a lower form in measures 5–8. No tonality is established in the fluid motion from F major to C♭ major; instead, a suspended atonal effect is achieved. The final C♭ sonority ultimately functions as a half-step neighbor chord above the B♭m11 destination and the recap of the head.

The recap of the head ⬚G⬚ is an abbreviated version of the earlier two-part twenty-four-measure form. Kessel and company re-join the arrangement as if it is the second time through the progression, with Edison's trumpet taking the lead. A repeat of the rising progression in measures 17–18 acts as a tag in measures 21–22. The piece ends in a contemporary vein with a final E♭maj7 chord instead of the customary dominant-seventh sonority of standard blues.

Fig. 26

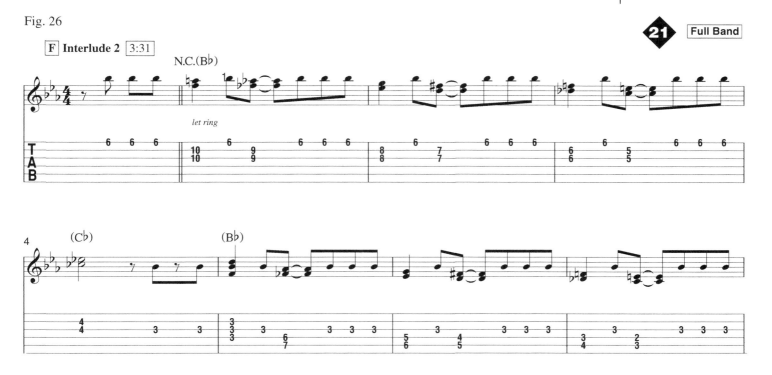

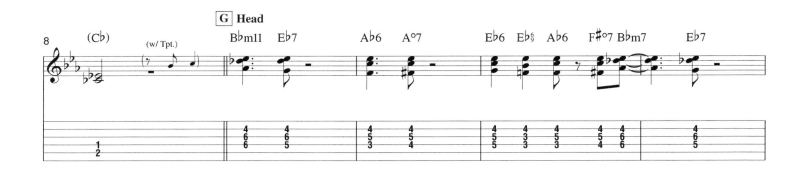

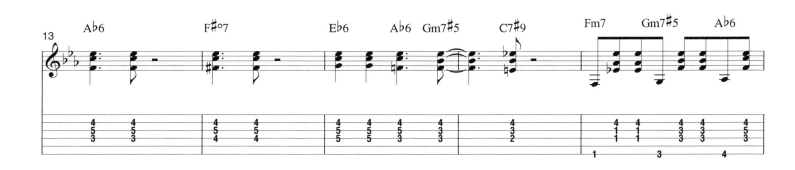

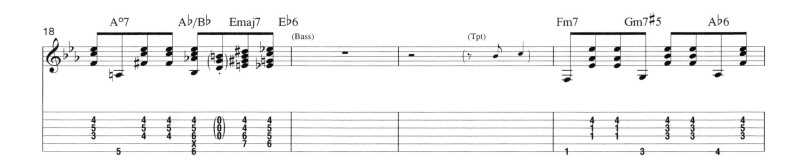

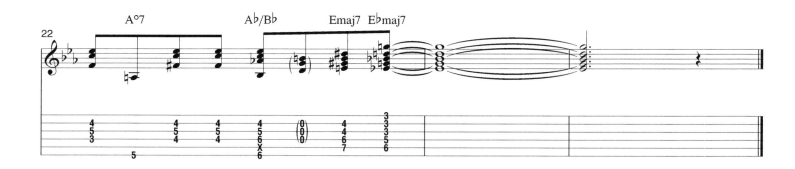

MINOR MOOD
(*The Poll Winners*)
By Barney Kessel

Figure 27—Head and Guitar Solo

"Minor Mood," a Barney Kessel original composition, is a leading tune from The Poll Winners' debut album—the first official guitar-led "super group" of combo jazz. The track was recorded in Los Angeles during the Contemporary studio sessions of March 18 and 19, 1957. In the head [A], Kessel presents a subtle but hypnotic fingerpicked theme in C minor accompanied only by Manne's sparse percussion part. In the second and third statements of the theme, Brown's bass enters and becomes the focal point, purveying a distinctive minor-mode blues riff over Kessel's now subordinate polyphonic background.

The roles and groove change for the first solo. At 0:32, Kessel begins an inventive five-chorus flight over a 12-bar blues in C minor.

1. [B] Kessel switches to plectrum style and quotes a classical theme in measures 17–20. He segues to minor-mode bop lines in measures 21–24 and caps off the chorus with three similar extended-arpeggio lines over A♭7, G7, and Cm in measures 26–28.

2. [C] Kessel plays chromaticized minor-mode melodies in measures 29–32. He applies the *whole-tone scale* in measure 33 to inflect the transition to Fm and create an ear-catching dominant-seventh-flat-five arpeggio, C7♭5. The cohesive rising line in measures 34–35 combines F minor and C minor scales.

3. [D] Kessel's rake-picking and slurred riffs distinguish measures 41–44. Kessel again inflects the move to Fm with C7 dissonance in measures 45–47. In the final section, measures 50–52, Kessel exploits three nearly identical shapes phrased in triplet rhythm for the A♭7–G7–Cm changes. This sound, based on extended *minor/major ninth arpeggios* of E♭m(maj9), Dm(maj9), and Cm(maj9), is a particularly useful dissonance and a staple of the hard bop genre.

4. [E] Kessel adopts a rhythmic approach with syncopation and staccato articulation of quarter notes in measures 54–58. He comps a brief chord figure in measures 59–60 for a pianistic touch between single-note lines.

5. [F] Kessel applies a modern Fm(maj7) arpeggio ascent in measure 70 and a swing-oriented Fm6 descent in measure 71 for an intriguing cross-generational combination. He closes with a variation of his incendiary Cm(maj9) lick of measure 52 as a final thought.

Fig. 27

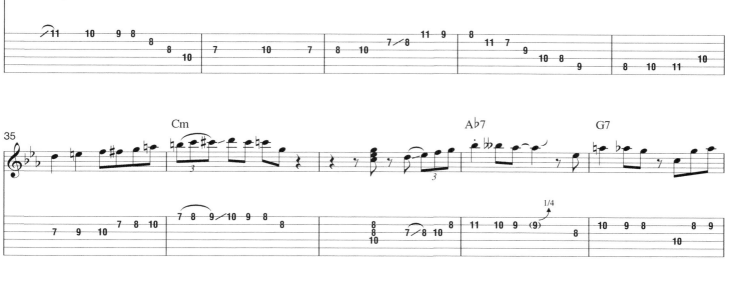

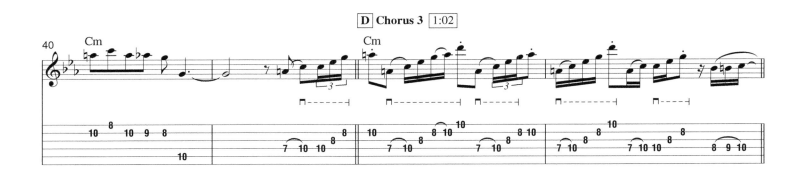

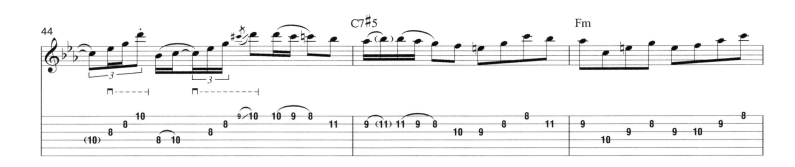

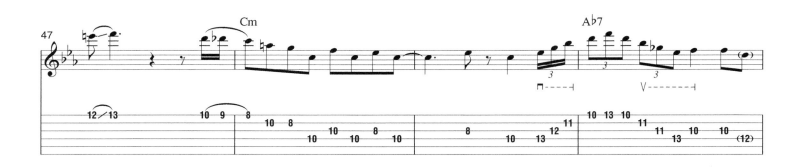

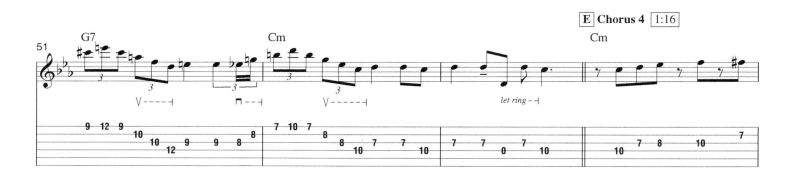

Figure 28—Interlude 1 and 2 and Recap

At 1:45, The Poll Winners begin a trading interlude, ⑤ and ⑥, featuring Brown's "lead bass" fills posed against Kessel's comping chord textures. This procedure prevails from measures 78 to 101. Note Kessel's use of varied block chords and triads, often slurred from a half step below, and typically strong rhythmic punctuation and placement in his homophonic phrases.

Kessel assumes the lead in the next interlude, ⑤ and ⑥. Here, he plays improvised chord-melody phrases in the manner of a jazz pianist. Note the use of block chord and triad textures for the most part in measures 102–113. He also develops smaller single-note, two-note, and three-note sounds in his contrapuntal riffs over Cm and Fm in measures 114–120. These are complimented by fuller chord punches in measures 116–117 and 120–121.

The theme recap resumes the earlier instrumentation of Kessel's polyphonic accompaniment with Brown's blues riffing and Manne's abstract percussion. The closing eight measures find the arrangement reverting to the opening texture of the head, with just Kessel's finger picking and sparse drum colors. The last sustained chord is a modern sonority, Cm(maj9), which personifies the song's title. This moody mysterious moment finds the trio playing together at the finale: Kessel's brushed strum, Manne's light cymbal hit and Brown's lingering bowed tone.

Fig. 28

FOREIGN INTRIGUE
(*The Poll Winners Ride Again*)
By Barney Kessel

Figure 29—Intro and Head

The Poll Winners Ride Again marked the second year of the trio's success and their growing pre-eminence among musicians, critics, and listeners. Recorded at Contemporary's LA studios on August 19 and 21, 1958, the album was a well-paced set containing evergreen standards like "Angel Eyes" and "Spring Is Here," pop tunes such as "Volare," unexpected novelty numbers like "When the Red Red Robin Comes Bob Bob Bobbin' Along" and "The Merry Go Round Broke Down," and new originals by Ray Brown and Barney Kessel.

One of the many strong suits of the Poll Winners was their ability to produce a kaleidoscopic musical vision with a minimum of instruments. "Foreign Intrigue" is a case in point. At the outset, this Kessel composition evokes the feeling of traversing a desert somewhere in North Africa or Arabia. Brown's pedal-point riff, conveying an exotic Phrygian melody, and Manne's percussion figures set a picturesque mood suggesting those distant lands and create a foundation for Kessel's sustaining subdued chord theme, which enters in the fifth measure of the intro A.

Kessel's atmospheric intro theme is made of harmonically-elusive triads from the *A Phrygian Mode* (A–B♭–C–D–E–F–G). Note the Am, B♭, C, G, and F triads played against an open high E string pedal tone. This strategy results in the uncommon dissonant sonority B♭♯11 and enriched chords G6 and Fmaj7.

In the head B, The Poll Winners take an abrupt turn into straight-ahead American jazz territory. In contrast to the floating ethnic mood of the intro, the head is taken at a brisk cut-time clip and exploits chord changes and melody indigenous to the modern jazz lexicon. Here, Kessel unfolds a hustling thirty-two-measure A–B–A–C theme in A minor. In its course, he delivers a characteristically multi-faceted statement of quick single-note melodies, chord punches, parallel 3rds, triads, and arpeggios.

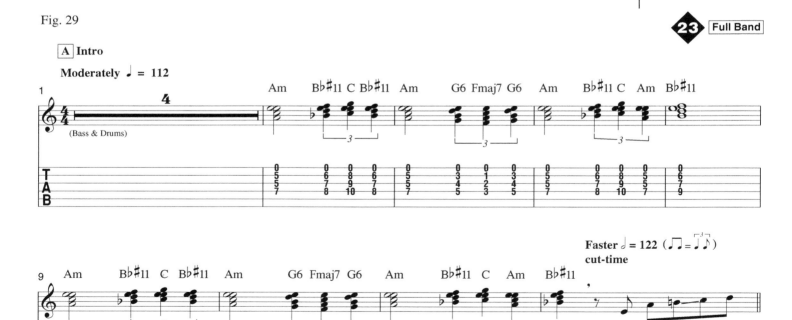

Fig. 29

Figure 30—Guitar Solo, Interlude, Recap and Outro

Kessel takes two choruses over the tune's thirty-two-measure form in his solo. His improvisations teem with signature licks. The first chorus C begins with modal, minor-blues, and jazz sounds in measures 27–33. The bop-inflected line in measures 41–42 defines the B7 chord and spells out an intriguing B7♭5 arpeggio in its descent. This is followed by an idiosyncratic riff of E+ and F♯+ arpeggios over E7, played with Kessel's patented rake-picking technique. He closes his first chorus in a blues vein, with string bends and pentatonic melody, in measures 57–60.

During the second chorus D, Kessel pursues varied chord textures. He plays a signature phrase of slurred block chords, triads, and dyads in measures 61–64 over the sustaining low E pedal point. This is complemented by an intriguing *tritone substitution* in measures 65–66; here Kessel plays a Dm7 pattern with raked arpeggios in measure 65 and repeats the pattern verbatim in measure 66 on the tritone level, A♭m7. The rising chromatic figure of 6/9 chords in measures 67–68 introduces quartal harmony. Kessel concludes the chordal section with a colorful episode of diatonic and chromatic third intervals over a low E pedal point in measures 69–72.

For the remainder of his solo, Kessel returns to single-note improvisation. His final long bop line in measures 85–88 exploits chromatic passing tones, stylistic enclosure figures, and dissonant extensions, like the *bi-tonal* diminished scale arpeggio (F–C–A–F♯) in measures 87–88 (beats 4–1). The solo concludes with bluesy string bending, staccato phrasing, and pentatonic melody in measures 89–92.

In the interlude E, Kessel alludes to the loose ethnic feeling and exotic modal dissonance of the intro with a brooding chord figure. Note his unique Am6/9 sonority and syncopated strum pattern, replete with ringing open strings, in measures 93–95. Through the progression, he modifies the harmony slightly (D♭7♯9 instead of G13) for smoother chromatic voice-leading. The second half of the progression is turned over to Manne for an eight-measure solo drum break.

The recap is a restatement of the head with slight variations and proceeds directly to a brief coda in free time. There, Kessel plays a descending modal progression of full sustaining chords. Note his five-and-six-note chords and open strings in the phrase. Several forms are facilitated with a *thumb-fretting technique*. The final dissonant sonority is Am(maj9), a favorite sound in the Kessel repertory. Here, Kessel expands the chord by adding a low E to the voicing, and Brown further colors the harmony by sounding a D note on his bass.

Fig. 30

* Play ahead of the beat.

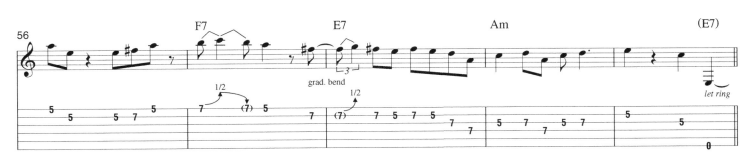

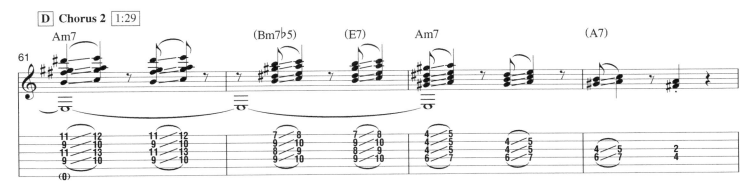